THE NORDIC TRANSLATION SERIES
Sponsored by
the Nordic Cultural Commission of
the Governments of
Denmark, Finland, Iceland, Norway, and Sweden

ADVISORY COMMITTEE
Einar Haugen, Harald S. Næss,
and Richard B. Vowles, Chairman

WE MURDERERS

VI MORDERE
Translated from the Danish by Einar Haugen
With an introduction by D. E. Askey

WE
MURDERERS

A PLAY IN THREE ACTS

Guðmundur Kamban

1970
The University of Wisconsin Press
Madison, Milwaukee, and London

Published by
The University of Wisconsin Press
Box 1379, Madison, Wisconsin 53701

The University of Wisconsin Press, Ltd.
27–29 Whitfield Street, London, W.1

Printed in the United States of America
By Kingsport Press, Inc., Kingsport, Tennessee

LC 70–98124; SBN 299–05511–6

CONTENTS

INTRODUCTION	ix
BIBLIOGRAPHY	xviii
LIST OF CHARACTERS	2
ACT I	3
ACT II	27
ACT III	51

INTRODUCTION

Guðmundur Kamban, an Icelandic playwright and novelist, spent most of his career in Denmark. Life was not rewarding for Kamban; his successes were never great enough to bring him the fame and fortune he sought. Numerous disappointments only enhanced his desire to continue striving toward his idealistic goals. His determination alone gave him the courage to withstand frequent criticism. Kamban was not a great literary figure, but his works do tell us something about his character and the character of the times in which he wrote. In order to facilitate an understanding of one of his better-known works, the play *We Murderers,* this introduction will provide a brief sketch of Guðmundur Kamban's life and literary development.

Kamban was born 8 June 1888 on a small farm just outside of Reykjavík, the capital of Iceland. He was one of several children of Jón Hallgrímsson and Guðný Jónsdóttir. His parents were poor, and his father's health was continually failing.

In spite of this, Jón was able to support his family with various part-time jobs in farming, fishing, and trading. When Jón was ill, Guðný would sometimes help out with the haymaking in addition to performing her household chores. They were industrious, hard-working people, and Guðmundur was later to show the same industriousness.

From 1904 to 1906 Kamban attended the Reykjavík Gymnasium, from which he graduated in 1910. During the intervening years (1906–1910) he worked as a journalist and studied on his own. Occasionally he would write a poem, and in 1906 his first book appeared. His most important writings at this time were three articles: "Surnames," "Philology and Style," and a review of a book by Jóhann Sigurjónsson. In "Surnames" he lashed out against the tendency in Iceland to favor, for reasons of nationalistic pride, the archaic practice of patronymics, which other Germanic nations had given up hundreds of years ago. He himself had dropped the patronymic "Jónsson" ("son of Jón") in favor of the surname "Kamban." In "Philology and Style" Kamban carried on his attack against excessive Icelandic nationalism by criticizing those who would consider any word as bad Icelandic, simply because it could not be found in ancient Icelandic texts. He pleaded for a new style in which the etymologies of words would be irrelevant,[1] rejected the stilted style of the sagas as inappropriate for modern expression, and claimed that the best literary language was the language of everyday speech, the language of feeling and emotion. This was Kamban the romantic—romantic in a restricted sense of the term. He had rejected the romanticism that accompanied strong Icelandic nationalism, but he (at least temporarily) held onto another form of romanticism that

1. In fact, Kamban was the first major Icelandic writer to put the word *takk* ("thanks"), used by Icelanders for decades (instead of the native Icelandic *þökk*), into the mouths of his characters. Cf. K. Albertson, "Þróun íslenzkunnar," *Skírnir*, 113 (1939): 38.

emphasized the beauty of human emotion and the power of human passion.

It is this latter form of romanticism that accounts for his favorable reception of the play *Bóndinn á Hrauni* (*The Farmer at Hraun*) by Jóhann Sigurjónsson, a romantic writer who heavily influenced Kamban's early thinking. Kamban was also influenced by the man he worked under as a journalist, Einar H. Kvaran, a popular author and editor at the time. Kvaran was a humanitarian, cosmopolitan, and political progressive. Kamban, who believed that man was essentially good and honest, protested, as we have seen, against narrow-minded nationalism in Iceland. Like many fellow Icelanders, he now prepared to seek new opportunities abroad. The world he later saw outside romantic Iceland was in desperate need of reform.

In 1910 Kamban set out for Denmark, where he studied philosophy and literature at the University of Copenhagen. He soon left school and turned to drama, which had been his greatest extracurricular interest. He wrote his first play *Hadda Padda* in 1912, but not until two years later did it appear in print. Hadda Padda is the nickname of a young girl, who is passionately in love with a boy named Ingólfur. In character she is very much like Norma in *We Murderers*. Ingólfur, however, falls in love with Kristrún, Hadda Padda's younger sister, who resembles Susan in *We Murderers*. In order to avenge herself on Ingólfur, Hadda Padda commits suicide right before his eyes. So the play ends. The famous Danish literary critic Georg Brandes lavishly praised *Hadda Padda*, and it was well received throughout Scandinavia.

In 1915 Kamban's second play *Wrestling before the King* appeared. Kamban had already been ranked among the better Dano-Icelandic writers, of whom the best known was Gunnar Gunnarsson. Both wrote in Danish in an effort to appeal to a larger reading audience than they would otherwise have enjoyed in Icelandic. Kamban's two plays are, however, set in

Iceland. They are romantic plays of love, jealousy, and revenge, dramatically centered around the character of a hard, passionate woman, who acts very much like the strong-minded heroine in old Icelandic sagas. The essence of *Hadda Padda* and *Wrestling before the King* is summed up in the words of Dúna Kvaran in Kamban's short story by the same name: "Love grows stronger in the heart that gives than in the heart that receives."

After his initial success Kamban began to seek new markets for his works. Because of the world war he could not go to Germany, and so he went to New York in the fall of 1915, where he stayed until 1917. It was during his stay in New York that he wrote the short story "Dúna Kvaran," which became the last work by Kamban the romantic. It appeared in 1916, the same year he married his Danish sweetheart Agnete Egeberg. Nevertheless, America was a personal disappointment to Kamban. For all his efforts to stage *Hadda Padda*, he merited nothing but an English translation of the play in 1917. He regretted that he had not been able to write in English, the international language. More than anything he was disturbed by what he felt was an unjust, inhuman treatment of the criminal in American society. Romantic love per se was no longer Kamban's main concern, for he had now begun to see society as the very obstacle to such love. If man did evil, it was evil only in the eyes of society, and directly as a result of society. Society condemned, in the name of law and order, what in fact it had caused. This double standard, this hypocrisy, this deception in society had the potential to destroy a basically good man. It destroyed Oscar Wilde, something for which Kamban would never forgive society. Now a bitter social critic, Kamban returned to Denmark.

New York provided Kamban with most of the material for his major works up until 1930. With *Marble* (1918), a play set in New York, he turned from romanticism to social realism, from wild passions against good and evil to idealistic protest against a decaying society. Like Oscar Wilde he satirized society's inhuman treatment of criminals. In *Ragnar Finnsson* (1922), his first novel, Kamban tells the story of an intelligent and sensitive young Icelander, Ragnar Finnsson, who seeks his fortune in the New World. Robbed of all his possessions, Ragnar resorts to stealing and is later imprisoned. As a youngster it was Ragnar's greatest desire, simple and naïve though it might be, to be good to everybody.

In *We Murderers* (1920) Kamban combined the social criticism of *Marble* and the passionate love of his first two plays into a careful psychological character study of an unhappily married woman in New York. The play is an imitation of the naturalistic works of Ibsen and Strindberg. Kamban does not explicitly condemn the society that will eventually punish Ernest for his crime, yet we do know where the author's sympathies lie. Kamban wants his audience to judge Ernest innocent, even though he is guilty before the law.

Norma is the typical strong-minded Kamban woman. Ernest is proud, sensitive, and hard-working. The cruelty and deception that each of them later shows are brought out in them through external environmental conditions, not through any natural tendency of their own to be cruel or deceptive. Each wants to be loved, and the conflict arises from two opposing expectations from love. Ernest asks Norma: "Hasn't it ever dawned on you . . . how different in their nature your and my love are?" Their differing expectations from love are conditioned by factors—in this case, persons—outside of their marriage. Norma has been influenced largely by her mother, Mrs. Dale, and Ernest by his friend Francis. These influences on both Norma and Ernest give rise to lies. Each deceives the other. Each puts the comforts of life or pride above being sincere and honest with oneself and one's partner. The cost of deception is the loss of love, or even more tragically, the loss of life. Ironically, however, Ernest and Norma love each other very much. In the words of Oscar Wilde, "each man kills the thing he loves."

In spite of encouragement by Brandes, *Marble* was never staged. *We Murderers*, on the other hand, was very well received. Kamban directed the play himself when it had its premiere on 2 March 1920 at the Dagmar Theatre, then one of the outstanding theaters in Copenhagen. It was also a great success in Oslo, where the leading role of Norma was played by the talented Norwegian actress Johanne Dybwad. But in Reykjavík, *We Murderers*, like *Hadda Padda* before it, was not successful.

In *The Arabian Tents* (1921), which is a less bitter satire than *We Murderers*, as well as in *Stars of the Desert* (1925), Kamban criticized the contemporary attitude toward sexual morality. Kamban felt that marriage, as a social institution, foolishly prevented a man from the expression of sincere extramarital love. In his article "Guðmundur Kamban" Stefán Einarsson wrote in reference to *The Arabian Tents:* "The difference between the marital conventions of the old and the young generation is that, though the ideal for both generations is marriage in love, the old generation emphasizes the marriage, whatever the state of the love, but the young generation emphasizes the love, whatever the state of the marriage."[2]

The Ambassador from Jupiter (1927) was the climax of Kamban's social criticism, which had become bitterly didactic. He attacked the emphasis in society on the cultivation of **the** mind at the expense of the heart. According to Einarsson in his *History of Icelandic Prose Writers*, "Kamban fastens his

2. Stefán Einarsson, "Guðmundur Kamban," *Tímarit Þjóðræknisfélag Íslendinga,* 14 (1932): 21.

hope for mankind on the passive resistance of conscience"
against social injustices.[3] Only kindness, sincerity, and honesty
can save the world. The ambassador from Jupiter says: "The
only way to reach that everlasting goal of happiness, for which
we all strive, is through complete, child-like sincerity." But
the didacticism was too strong, and the play was harshly criticized for excessive preaching. In the spring of 1927, at a time
when there was great discussion about building a national
theater in Iceland, Kamban tried to convince the Dramatic
Society of Reykjavík to present *The Ambassador from Jupiter*.
His attempt failed, and so at his own expense he financed the
production of the play in Reykjavík and played the ambassador himself. At the same time he restaged *We Murderers*.
Both plays were failures. Again Kamban was deeply disap-
pointed, as he had been in New York, and this disappointment had a great effect on his later literary development. In
Morgunblaðið (Reykjavík), 22 May 1927, Kamban wrote:

> I wanted to show foreign nations that Iceland had a modern
> culture. I wanted to do that in my first two plays by setting the
> drama in the cultural environment of Iceland. In my later works
> the action takes place in the cultural environment of large cities
> —the environment of international culture. The last link in this
> chain is *The Ambassador from Jupiter*, originating out of post-
> war Western civilization, transcending time and space. . . .
> Now I can turn back to my own country, where there is a
> wealth of subject material.

For the next two years Kamban read a great deal of Icelandic history, where he struck upon the seventeenth-century
love story of Ragnheiður Brynjólfsdóttir and Daði Halldórsson, which became the basis of his historical novels, the
Skálholt tetralogy (1930–1932). When Ragnheiður's father,

3. Stefán Einarsson, *History of Icelandic Prose Writers 1800–1940*
(Ithaca, N.Y.: Cornell University Press, 1948), pp. 142–143. (= *Islandica* 32–33.)

Brynjólfur, one of the bishops at Skálholt during the seventeenth century, realized that the love affair between his daughter and Daði, who also lived at Skálholt, might develop into a scandal, he forced Ragnheiður to swear that she would not have any sexual relations with Daði. Ragnheiður took the oath, but in obstinate defiance of her father's will she slept with Daði. Kamban portrayed the love between Ragnheiður and Daði as both spiritual and physical. The portrayal of physical love relations in print was a bold undertaking for Kamban's times, when the beauty of love was considered to consist essentially in its spiritual aspects. Through the strong-minded characters of Bishop Brynjólfur and his daughter, Kamban tried to contrast seventeenth and twentieth-century moral standards. Brynjólfur is the stern Puritanical churchman to whom love means a giving and understanding heart. Ragnheiður is one of the young generation to whom love means an understanding heart *and* a warm caress—a fusion of both the spiritual and the physical. One Icelandic historian criticized Kamban for having misrepresented seventeenth-century Iceland in the Skálholt novels, especially through his efforts to bring in twentieth-century moral standards. But we must remember: Kamban wanted to transcend time. He shifted, for example, from the use of the past tense in the novel *Ragnar Finnsson* to the use of the historical present in *Skálholt*. This shift was an implicit transcendence of time. Kamban felt that nothing changes; this feeling justified his desire to transcend time as well as space. The paradox[4] is that Kamban opposed the idea of art for art's sake; art for him was the means to express his humanitarian, cosmopolitan, and progressive ideas. But if nothing changes, what does social criticism avail?

During the 1920's Kamban had enjoyed some popularity in Germany. With *Skálholt* he became even more popular there.

4. Kristinn E. Andrésson, *Íslenzkar nútímabókmenntir 1918–1948* (Reykjavík: Mál og Menning, 1949), pp. 229–230.

The historical novel *I See a Wondrous Land* (1936) was written in Berlin. It is an adventure story about Icelandic viking explorations of Greenland and America. Political trends in Germany at the time no doubt influenced his writing. *I See a Wondrous Land* is dedicated to the Nordic Spirit. Kamban did not stay in Germany, but returned to Copenhagen, where he remained for five years. He was unpopular in Denmark because of his German connections and returned to Germany in 1943. His stay this time was very short, and he was soon back in Copenhagen. On 5 May 1945 the Allies were celebrating a victory in Denmark. That same day three members of the Danish underground approached Kamban; he was suspected of German sympathies. Kamban resisted arrest and was shot in the head—a tragic and ironic fate for a critic of social injustice.

D. E. ASKEY

Cambridge, Massachusetts
July 1969

BIBLIOGRAPHY

BY GUÐMUNDUR KAMBAN[1]

Úr dularheimum (*From Occult Worlds*). Reykjavík: Ísafold, 1906. Tales.

"Review of Jóhann Sigurjónsson's *Bóndinn á Hrauni*," *Ísafold* (Reykjavík), 5 December 1908.

"Ættarnöfn" ("Surnames"), *Skírnir* 82 (1908): 164–177. Essay.

"Málfræði og stíll" ("Philology and Style"), *Ísafold* (Reykjavík), 14 August 1909. Essay.

"Faxi," *Skírnir* 88 (1914): 250–255. Short story. Danish: "Faxi," *Tilskueren* 31, sec. 2 (1914): 165–169. Later appeared as the first chapter of *Ragnar Finnsson*.

Hadda Padda. Reykjavík: Ólafur Thors, 1914. Play. Danish:

1. Several individual poems appeared in various Icelandic magazines and newspapers between 1905 and 1934. Because of their relative unimportance they are not cited here.

Hadda Padda. Copenhagen: Gyldendal, 1914. English: *Hadda Padda*. Translated by Sadie Luise Peeler, with foreword by Georg Brandes. New York: A. A. Knopf, 1917.

Kongeglimen (Wrestling before the King). Copenhagen: Gyldendal, 1915. Play.

"Dúna Kvaran," *Skírnir* 90 (1916): 378–390. Short story. Danish: "Duna Kvaran," *Tilskueren* 34, sec. 1 (1917): 128–138.

Marmor (Marble). Copenhagen: V. Pio, 1918. Play.

"Vondafljót," *Eimreiðin* 25 (1919): 160–165. Short story. *Vi Mordere (We Murderers)*. Copenhagen: V. Pio, 1920. Play.

"Vizka hefndarinnar" ("The Wisdom of Revenge"), *Skírnir* 94 (1920): 81–89. Short story.

"Þegar konur fyrirgefa—" ("When Women Forgive—"), *Eimreiðin* 26 (1920): 193–200. Short story.

De arabiske Telte (The Arabian Tents). Copenhagen: V. Pio, 1921. Play.

Ragnar Finnsson. Copenhagen: V. Pio, 1922. Novel. Icelandic: *Ragnar Finnsson*. Reykjavík: Þorsteinn Gíslason, 1922. German: *Ragnar Finnsson*. Translated by Else von Hollander-Lossow. Braunschweig: Georg Westermann, 1925. The beginning of Chapter 3 appeared as "Jugendzeit" in *Wie und was aus dem Schrifttum der Zeitgenossen*, no. 18. Braunschweig: Georg Westermann, 1930.

Det sovende Hus (The Sleeping House). Copenhagen: Hasselbalch, 1925. Novel. German: *Das schlafende Haus*. Translated by Else von Hollander-Lossow. Braunschweig: Georg Westermann, 1926. Icelandic: *Meðan húsið svaf*. Reykjavík: Helgafell, 1948.

Ørkenens Stjerner (Stars of the Desert). Copenhagen: Hasselbalch, 1925. Play.

Sendiherrann frá Júpíter (The Ambassador from Jupiter). Reykjavík: Ársæll Árnason, 1927. Play.

"Daði Halldórsson og Ragnheiður Brynjólfsdóttir," *Skírnir* 103 (1929): 36–83. Essay.

"Leikhús Íslands" ("An Icelandic Theater"), *Lesbók Morgun-blaðiðsins* 4 (1929): 217–219, 227–230, 233–234. Essay.

"Oscar Wilde," *Iðunn* 13 (1929): 193–228. Essay.

"Reykjavíkurstúlkan" ("The Reykjavík Girl"), *Eimreiðin* 35 (1929): 215–232. Essay.

"Á Alþingi 1631" ("At the Althing in 1631"), *Iðunn* 14 (1930): 1–32. Short story.

"Hallgrímur Pétursson járnsmiður" ("Hallgrímur Pétursson the Blacksmith"), *Iðunn* 14 (1930): 209–243. Short story. This and the preceding later appeared as chapters in *Skálholt*.

Skálholt I, Jomfru Ragnheiður. Copenhagen: Hasselbalch, 1930. Novel. Icelandic: *Skálholt I, Jómfrú Ragnheiður*. Reykjavík: Ísafold, 1930.

Skálholt II, Mala domestica . . . . Copenhagen: Hasselbalch, 1931. Novel. Icelandic: *Skálholt II, Mala domestica* . . . . Reykjavík: Ísafold, 1931. German: *Die Jungfrau auf Skalholt*. Translation of *Skálholt I* and *II* by Edzard H. Schaper. Leipzig: Insel-Verlag, 1934 (and 1938). English: *The Virgin of Skalholt*. Translation of *Skálholt I* and *II* by Evelyn C. Ramsden. Boston: Little, Brown & Co., 1935.

Skálholt III, Hans Herredom. Copenhagen: Hasselbalch, 1932. Novel. Icelandic: *Skálholt III, Hans Herradómur*. Reykjavík: Ísafold, 1934.

Skálholt IV, Quod felix . . . . Copenhagen: Hasselbalch, 1932. Novel. Icelandic: *Skálholt IV, Quod felix* . . . . Reykjavík: Ísafold, 1935. German: *Der Herrscher auf Skalholt*. Translation of *Skálholt III* and *IV* by Edzard H. Schaper. Leipzig: Insel-Verlag, 1938 (and 1943).

30. Generation (*30th Generation*). Copenhagen: Hasselbalch, 1933. Novel. German: *Die dreissigste Generation*. Translated by Helm. Giese. Berlin: Holle & Co., 1937.

Davíð skygni. Translation of Jonas Lie's *Den fremsynte*. Reykjavík: Félagsprentsmiðjan, 1934.

På Skálholt (*At Skálholt*). Copenhagen: Hasselbalch, 1934.
Play.

Jeg ser et stort skønt Land. Copenhagen: Gyldendal, 1936.
Novel. German: *Ich seh ein grosses schönes Land.* Trans-
lated by Edzard H. Schaper. Leipzig: Insel-Verlag, 1937.
English: *I See a Wondrous Land.* New York: Putnam, 1938.
Also translated by Evelyn C. Ramsden. London: Nicholson
& Watson, 1938. Icelandic: *Vítt sé ég land og fagurt.* 2 vols.
Reykjavík: Helgafell, 1945–1946.

Derfor skilles vi (*Therefore We Part*), unpublished. Play.
Based on *De arabiske Telte,* staged 1939.

Grandezza. Copenhagen: Gyldendal, 1941. Play.

Komplekser (*Complexes*). Copenhagen: Gyldendal, 1941.
Play. Icelandic: *Vöf,* unpublished; staged 1941.

Kvalitetsmennesket (*Man of Quality*). Copenhagen: Gyldendal, 1941. Essays.

Hvide Falke (*White Falcons*). Copenhagen: Munksgaard,
1944. Anthology of Icelandic poetry in Danish translation.

ABOUT GUÐMUNDUR KAMBAN

Andrésson, Kristinn E. *Íslenzkar nútímabókmenntir 1918–1948.*
Reykjavík: Mál og Menning, 1949.

Brandes, Georg. "Gudmundur Kamban: Hadda Padda," *Tilskueren* 31, sec. 1 (1914): 401–412.

Einarsson, Stefán. "Guðmundur Kamban," *Tímarit Þjóðræknisfélag Íslendinga* 14 (1932): 7–29.

———. *History of Icelandic Prose Writers 1800–1940.* Ithaca,
N.Y.: Cornell University Press, 1948. (= *Islandica* 32–33).

———. *History of Icelandic Literature.* New York: The Johns
Hopkins Press for the American-Scandinavian Foundation,
1957.

Ellehauge, Martin. *Det danske Skuespil efter Verdenskrigen.* Copenhagen: Munksgaard, 1933.

Hall, Gunnar. *Íslendingabók: Æviágrip og brautryðjendasaga merkra Íslendinga.* Reykjavík: Leiftur, 1958.

Kress, Helga. "Guðmundur Kamban, æskuverk og ádeilur." Thesis for cand. mag. degree, University of Iceland, 1969. Forthcoming as vol. 29 in Steingrímur J. Þorsteinsson, ed., *Studia Islandica* (Reykjavík: Háskóli Islands, 1970).

Levy, Louis. "Tre Skuespil," *Tilskueren* 37, sec. 1 (1920): 298–299.

Ree, Örnulf. "En islandsk Dramatiker (Gudmundur Kamban: Vi Mordere)," *Nordisk Tidskrift för Vetenskap, Konst och Industri* (1921), pp. 39–42.

Sigurbjörnsson, Lárus. "Guðmundur Kamban," *Skírnir* 119 (1945): 23–35.

Þorsteinsson, Steingrímur J. "Islandsk Skuespildigtning og Skuespilkunst." Stencilled. Lecture held at the Sixth Nordic Theatrical Congress, at the National Theatre of Iceland, Reykjavík, 4 June 1956.

WE MURDERERS

CHARACTERS

ERNEST MCINTYRE, *inventor*
NORMA MCINTYRE, *his wife*
SUSAN DALE, *her sister*
LILLIAN DALE, *their mother*
FRANCIS MCLEAN
EDWARD RATTIGAN
KATE, *a colored woman*

Place: NEW YORK
Time: THE PRESENT [1920]
Between the acts: ONE NIGHT, THIRTEEN DAYS

ACT I

Livingroom in the McIntyre home. Furniture late Empire, well-styled and solid, not showy. Door on left leading to the hall, and another in the rear to Ernest's study. Windows right. Between the windows a sofa with a table and chairs before it. In the corner between the window and the door heating ducts, concealed in the wall. Right front, near the wall, an old Chinese chiffoniere, tastefully inlaid with mother of pearl and silver, with a mirror on top, behind four low pillars. A grand piano left front. Bookcases to the left of each door. Large and small bouquets of flowers around the room.

(*Norma sits behind the table on the right, pouring coffee and liqueurs. Mrs. Dale is going over to a chair on the left of the table. She is fifty or a little over, small and thin, inconspicuous, with a constant smile on her lips.*)

NORMA: Sit down, mother.

MRS. DALE: Thank you. (*Sits down on the chair.*) It was a lovely evening, Norma dear. First the opera and now your

3

dinner. I think Wagner's music is the most charming I know. Where do you buy your olives, Norma? And what a salad you make! Mmm.

(*The laughter of two men is heard from the study.*)

NORMA: Curaçao or DOM?

MRS. DALE: Curaçao, please . . . Why don't we move into the other room? It's nicer to be all together.

NORMA: We can hear the telephone better in here.

MRS. DALE: Are you expecting a call?

NORMA: Just Susan. I'm expecting her to call and say how sorry she is that she can't come.

MRS. DALE: Oh no, Norma. That wouldn't be like Susan at all.

NORMA: It wasn't very nice of her not to come here for dinner. On my birthday . . . Is she out with Mr. Bowman?

MRS. DALE: I don't think so. Tonight I think she was going out with the Clifford girls.

NORMA: Do you really believe that? You're pretty naïve, mother. Haven't you found out yet who the Clifford girls are?

MRS. DALE: Yes, they've been to tea at my house twice. They are daughters of one of the biggest wine merchants in Boston, a very rich family, and very sweet young girls.

NORMA: The Clifford girls are—Mr. Arthur Wallace, New York City, owner of a big ceramics plant in New Jersey, six feet tall, balding on top, with a pair of sharp mustaches that stand out like the hands of a clock. (*With an illustrative gesture.*) At a quarter to three.

MRS. DALE: It isn't nice of you, Norma, to talk that way about your sister.

NORMA: About my brother-in-law, you mean.

MRS. DALE: I'm afraid he'll never be that. His greatest wish is to marry her. But Susan is so kind that she wouldn't take him away from his wife and two children.

4

NORMA: Well, then Mrs. Wallace ought to be delighted. Has she returned the call?

MRS. DALE: Heavens, Norma. Susan can't help it that Mr. Wallace is in love with her.

NORMA: No, she just accepts one expensive gift after the other from him—to keep him away.

MRS. DALE: Well, that isn't right of Susan, I'll admit. But she's in a very difficult position. You have no idea how unpleasant it is for her to accept such expensive gifts. Imagine, just the other day he said to her that if she broke her friendship with him, he would die of grief.

NORMA: And the same is true, of course, of Mr. Bowman and Dr. Lippincott. You know what, mother: Susan could pamper her need for luxury in a much more pleasant way. Since she can rescue so many people from death, she ought to make a deal with a life insurance company and get them to pay her.

MRS. DALE: You've turned so bitter, Norma. So awfully bitter. That's what Susan says too. She says it's your marriage that has made you this way.

NORMA (shakes her head, half in despair): Those two months in Florida—what a delightful time that was. Nobody to criticize or to admonish me. When you don't like me, you and Susan blame it on my marriage—and Ernest blames it on my upbringing.

MRS. DALE: Your upbringing! And you stand for that?

NORMA: For one thing, he says that when I was little nobody taught me to shut the door behind me.

MRS. DALE: Good Lord, how petty can men get?

NORMA (almost proud): He says that my strength of character will continue to be deficient as long as I forget to shut the door behind me.

MRS. DALE: And you've been married to this man for nine years!

5

NORMA: I've been sad many a day. (*Joins her hands behind her head.*) And there's never been an evening that I wished I hadn't married him . . . Here comes Susan.

MRS. DALE: Is anyone opening the door for her?

NORMA: Ernest went out. (*Silence.*)

SUSAN (*comes rushing in from the left, leaves the door half open, and goes right over to the chiffoniere*): Good evening. Please excuse me, Norma, for coming so late. But I always have such a time getting rid of the Cliffords. (*Stops before the mirror, takes out a compact from her stocking top, and fixes her makeup quite thoroughly.*) Awfully nice kids, but just a little bit tiresome.

(*Mrs. Dale gets up from old habit to close the door.*)

NORMA (*very seriously*): Susan—

SUSAN: Yes.

NORMA: Don't you think just the same that you would miss the Cliffords if you didn't have them?

SUSAN (*with a quick glance at the door*): Do you think it is fun for me to stay home—alone with mother?

NORMA (*silent a moment, gets up*): No.

(*Mrs. Dale returns to the chair where she was sitting.*)

SUSAN (*takes a last look at herself in the mirror, and goes over to the others*): Well, now tell me what you got, Norma. Did you have a real harvest? Oh, I know about the flowers, mother told me. But the gifts—what did you get?

NORMA (*over to a little table between the piano and the door*): Here's the traditional box of chocolates from Aunt Harriet. And there's a selection of Browning from my brother-in-law.

SUSAN (*quickly picks up the book*): In nile-green leather, isn't that charming. And what else?

NORMA (*lifts up a thin cardboard box*): This is from Mrs. Beauchamp, a negligee.

MRS. DALE (*unfolding the negligee*): Isn't it enchanting?

NORMA: Two pair of stockings from my sister-in-law.
SUSAN (*picks up a little electric night lamp*): This owl is awfully sweet. Who sent you that?
NORMA: I got that from Mr. McLean. That made me very happy. Then I got some lovely carnations, writing paper, and two dozen handkerchiefs from mother. And then your gift, Susan. Thanks ever so much. (*Kisses her cheek.*) You couldn't have picked anything I would have been happier about.
SUSAN: Oh, that was nothing. But what did you get from your husband?
NORMA (*as she goes over to the chiffoniere and takes with her a small box which she opens and lays aside*): The huge basket of orchids—my favorite flowers.
MRS. DALE (*over to a small flower table in the left rear corner*): Here it is.
NORMA (*standing before the chiffoniere, where she puts on her arm a wristwatch which she has taken out of the box*): Just look at this, Susan!
SUSAN (*over to Norma*): You have a beautiful gift for your thirtieth birthday, I'll bet.
NORMA (*turns around, her hands behind her back*): Yes.
SUSAN: What is it?
(*Norma holds the hand with the watch up for her to look at.*)
SUSAN: It's fabulous . . . It suits your hand.
NORMA: It's from Tiffany's. Gold plate. A French model, but doesn't it remind you of an old rococo piece? (*Skims it across her chin.*) I love it.
MRS. DALE: And it's so simple.
SUSAN: Maybe a trifle too big.
NORMA: No, Susan, you haven't noticed the engraving. It couldn't be any other size. Look!
SUSAN (*takes her hand in both of her own*): Well . . . Yes . . . Maybe.
NORMA (*stares at Susan's wrist, which is adorned with a*

7

huge bracelet of platinum, inlaid with large sapphires in ellipses of brilliants. An expression of distress falls on Norma's face as she withdraws her hand): When did you get that?

SUSAN: Today . . . Do you like it?

NORMA: It's worth a fortune.

MRS. DALE *(overcome by enthusiasm)*: My, Susan! That's a real treasure.

NORMA: Who gave you that?

SUSAN: One doesn't ask such questions . . . Why are you smiling?

NORMA: I was just going to say that you get your gifts cheaply. I smiled because I was mistaken.

SUSAN: I don't think it's anything for you to stick your nose into.

MRS. DALE: I don't feel you should say that about Susan. Don't you remember—she was only seventeen when Lord Kitton pulled out his necktie pin with a rare pearl in it and offered it to her for a single kiss. That was a real temptation for a seventeen-year-old girl. But Susan has always been highminded, and she refused the offer. *(A little coquettishly.)* After all, she couldn't very well accept such an expensive gift just for giving him a kiss.

SUSAN: Oh, stop that nonsense.

MRS. DALE: How dare you talk to me that way?

SUSAN *(over to the table without answering)*: Norma, I'm taking a glass of DOM.

NORMA: Go ahead.

(Mrs. Dale stands still for a moment, and then sails into the study.)

SUSAN *(puts down the half-emptied glass and lies down on the sofa)*: Don't you think you would like to trade with me now, Norma?

NORMA: No. *(Goes over to the chair on the left of the table and sits down.*) Strange of you to ask. Are you as happy as all that?

SUSAN: As happy as all that? (*Laughs.*) Yes, I think so.

NORMA: Well, maybe.

SUSAN (*lifts herself on her elbow*): Aren't you tired of being poor after almost ten years?

NORMA: I don't think I need to enlighten you about that. But why talk about it? It's so hopeless.

SUSAN: How do you manage to be so well-dressed all the time—with such a small income?

NORMA: Am *I* well dressed? . . . Do you think so?

SUSAN: You most certainly are. You have plenty of clothes.

NORMA: I just have to look decent in my clothes. It's my nature, and nothing can change it. But it costs me a terrible lot of self-reproach. Ernest is so good to me. But it hurts me to take every cent that he might save just to dress myself up. As for him—it struck me just yesterday, when we were walking down the street together, that he is almost poorly dressed.

SUSAN: I'm sorry for you, Norma. What did you get in return for your beauty and your youth?

NORMA: A husband I wouldn't trade for anybody else.

SUSAN: You certainly thought, when you married him, that he would have a much more brilliant future ahead of him.

NORMA: Yes, I did. He didn't have a cent. But he had made three big inventions and he had the patents in his hands . . . And then they stole them away from him.

SUSAN: But this only shows how impractical he is as a businessman.

NORMA: I don't know. He had taken out supplementary patents on all of them. But still they managed to get around them. And the people who used his invention for taking out a patent on the improvements got rich. We were left with the pains, just as poor as ever.

SUSAN: Patent on the improvements: isn't that what I said? His inventions couldn't be used as they were. That's what makes him impractical. Everybody says so.

NORMA: Only people who don't know what they're talking about say so. Every big newspaper in New York is making two hundred thousand dollars a year on their ad contests. This was Ernest's idea exactly, just as he laid it before Mr. Kingstone in the presence of two famous lawyers. Just the same he lost the lawsuit when Mr. Kingstone stole the idea. If Ernest was impractical, so was Mr. Kingstone, for he couldn't patent the idea, either. It's hard enough to protect physical objects. It's impossible to protect a mere idea, no matter how good it is.

SUSAN (*emptying her glass*): There *are* inventors who earn piles of money. They don't all let their patents get stolen.

NORMA: Only one out of ten has the capital to protect them, either by helping to support the production, or—well, or by luck. By luck I mean that they meet up with people who aren't bandits.

SUSAN (*smiling*): Do you need capital to have luck?

NORMA: Exactly.

SUSAN: No, you can't make me believe that. Ernest would have done better at the age of thirty-four than just being a clever experimenter in an electrical laboratory if he really had been a foresighted and practical businessman. That is the hope you have been living on so far.

NORMA: If in my heart of hearts I should doubt that my husband really had the abilities that he says he has and that he believes in with such burning conviction, then—

SUSAN: What then?

NORMA: I don't doubt, Susan.

SUSAN: Yes, you do. You said earlier that your future was so hopeless. I can see it in you, Norma, now lately, that you have lost your faith in life. Especially since you came back home. You imagined that a two-month vacation in Florida would cheer you up. But you came back twice as dissatisfied.

NORMA: I wouldn't have missed that trip for anything in the world. It's the only joy I've had for many, many years.

SUSAN: I would have guessed it was the only grief you had had, to judge by your humor since you came home.

NORMA (*looks up hastily*): Do you say so, too? Well, who knows . . . Sometimes grief comes to people in lonely majesty. Joy never comes alone. (*With sudden change of mood.*) Don't you understand? To ride when you feel like it. To drive long trips when you feel like it. To fly when you feel like it.

SUSAN (*with a trace of a scornful smile*): No, I don't underderstand. *Now* you can kiss your husband when you feel like it.

NORMA: You don't think I missed Ernest while I was in Florida. You're wrong. But to miss out on all the comforts of life just because you love a man—that is what infuriates me.

SUSAN: You don't need to, if others can furnish them . . . By the way, you're still flying with Mr. Rattigan since you got back, aren't you?

NORMA: Yes, still.—Susan . . .

SUSAN: Yes.

NORMA: Can you understand why we never flew when we were children?

SUSAN: It's very difficult to understand. But if you really collect your wits for a few months and make a thorough study of the history of aviation, you'll gradually discover the reason.

NORMA (*smiling*): Yes, of course . . . Do you remember the fairytale grandmother told us about the prince who came every night in a swan's guise to the woman he loved in secret? Isn't it marvelous that man's inventiveness gradually turns all our fairytales into reality?

SUSAN: As far as love is concerned, man's inventiveness turns

11

reality into a fairytale. Where in the world have I put my bag? (*Gets up.*) Oh, I guess I forgot it by the mirror. (*Goes out in the hall and leaves the door ajar.*)

ERNEST (*enters from rear and leaves the door wide open. He is in evening dress. Pale, quiet, and decisive in manner. He goes over to Norma and says in a loud voice, so the guests will hear it*): Now we can't get along without the birthday child any longer.

NORMA (*gets up, puts her hand on his arm, and says coquettishly, without lowering her voice*): Is she his own little girl?

ERNEST (*becomes a trifle nervous and hushes her*): Oh— why talk so loudly, they heard you.

NORMA: Not a person can hear us.

ERNEST (*in a low voice, with brows knit*): You're shouting, Norma. Susan is out in the hall, and your mother and Francis are in the study.

NORMA: You're ridiculously sensitive.

ERNEST: No, I just can't stand it that we expose our feelings in the presence of others. Oh, why doesn't *she* close the door behind her, either?

NORMA: This time you left the door open, too.

ERNEST: You don't distinguish reasons, Norma. When you've invited your guests into the livingroom, you can't slam the door in front of their noses.

NORMA: Do I have to listen to reproaches this evening?

ERNEST: No, no, no. So, now we'll call them in.

NORMA: Kiss me first.

(*Ernest hushes her again and pulls back just a little.*)

NORMA: It doesn't matter what I do, it's always wrong.

ERNEST: No, no. (*Takes a quick look at both doors. Kisses her forehead. Goes over to the door in the rear wall.*) Please, come in. (*Over to the hall.*) Aren't you coming in, Susan? (*Goes into the study.*) Then we'll take the whiskey in here.

MRS. DALE (*enters from the rear*): Shouldn't I get something to wrap around your shoulders, Norma? Be careful about your stomach catarrh.

NORMA: Oh, mother. You know how you irritate me with your constant prattling. Please sit down now, mother.

(*Mrs. Dale starts to answer, but gives it up and sits down in an easy chair, just as Francis enters from the rear and Susan from the left.*)

FRANCIS (*in his mid-thirties, with a clear expression, not entirely free from severity*): Good evening, Miss Dale.

SUSAN: Good evening, Mr. McLean. (*Gives him her hand.*) How did you enjoy the opera?

FRANCIS: Thank you, I missed you on my left side. On the right I had the pleasure of having your mother.

(*Mrs. Dale sends him a grateful smile.*)

SUSAN: Can I make up for it—here on the sofa? (*She sits.*) (*Francis bows and sits down beside her.*)

NORMA (*over by the flower table, enjoying the fragrance of red roses, looks at Mr. McLean with a sarcastic smile*): Well, is the sofa satisfactory?

FRANCIS (*making himself comfortable*): The sofa—yes, I really think it will do a lot—to make up for it.

(*Susan giggles.*)

ERNEST (*enters from the study with whiskey, glasses, and cigars on a small tray, which he places on the table, and then closes the door*): Aren't you coming over here, Norma?

NORMA: Yes. (*Continues to care for the flowers.*)

ERNEST (*sits down by the far end of the table and starts to prepare the drinks*): Say when, Francis.

FRANCIS: Thanks . . . Isn't it a little warm here?

SUSAN: Whew, its suffocating. Only for Negroes.

FRANCIS: Or Eskimos.

SUSAN: Why Eskimos?

FRANCIS: Well—

ERNEST (*fills the glasses with soda*): I'll shut off the heat.

NORMA (*goes over to the ducts*): I'll do it.

ERNEST: Thank you, Norma. (*Lifts his glass and drinks with Francis.*)

FRANCIS (*to Susan*): Haven't you heard the story of the Danish parson in Greenland who preached the faith to the Eskimos? To begin with the church was filled. But when he began to explain to them how hot it was in the dwellings of the damned, the Eskimos stopped going to church. They all wanted to go to hell.

NORMA (*sitting down by the table*): You should come to our house more often than you do, Mr. McLean. You always bring laughter and sunshine with you.

ERNEST (*in the same tone*): —and chocolate! Yes, you really ought to come more often, Francis.

FRANCIS: There you hear it, Mrs. McIntyre. Ernest McIntyre is a dangerous rival.

MRS. DALE (*half anxious, half forward*): A person never knows.

(*Ernest appears to have discovered her presence for the first time.*)

FRANCIS: Oh, *I* know Ernest. From his school days. His wit and humor were renowned. He brightened up any company he joined. Yes, Mrs. McIntyre, you spoke the word: he brought laughter and sunshine with him wherever he went. (*Mrs. Dale turns around on her chair and starts studying the paintings on the left wall through her lorgnette. Susan turns in the sofa and lets her eyes glide over the paintings on the right wall.*)

ERNEST: For heaven's sake, Francis, you mustn't start praising me. It stirs up such a burning interest in art in my mother-in-law and my sister-in-law. And I'm not sure that our paintings can withstand their criticism.

SUSAN (*pointedly*): It might just have happened that you had given your wife a new painting.

FRANCIS (*suddenly*): Have you been flying today, Mrs. McIntyre?

NORMA: No.

ERNEST: Haven't you—?

NORMA: Yes, yes . . . I didn't pay any attention to what you were asking about. Yes, I was in the air for over an hour. First we flew over New York, back and forth. Then to Washington and back home.

ERNEST: To Boston, you mean.

NORMA: No, to Washington.

ERNEST: Yes, of course, I remembered wrong. (*Sips from his glass.*)

MRS. DALE (*to Ernest*): Don't you think it's fun for Norma that she got acquainted with Mr. Rattigan in Florida?

ERNEST: Yes, great fun. (*Looks hatefully at her.*)

MRS. DALE: I think it's so nice of him to—

NORMA (*interrupting in a loud voice*): Mother, don't you want a pillow behind your back? Oh, Susan, would you please hand it to me?

SUSAN: Here you are. (*Tosses the pillow over to her mother.*)

FRANCIS: I knew Mr. Rattigan's father for a while. He was a very pleasant person.

MRS. DALE: Oh you did, the old soap manufacturer? He died insane.

FRANCIS: I never heard that.

MRS. DALE (*afraid to maintain an opinion*): No, well, that is—slightly insane.

NORMA: I think his son has a touch of the same. He can get insanely angry.

ERNEST: Have you been exposed to it?

NORMA: No, of course not. (*Half jestingly.*) I'm only exposed to that in my marriage.

FRANCIS: Ernest isn't hot-tempered.

NORMA: No? You aren't married to him.

15

ERNEST: You aren't married to Mr. Rattigan either.

SUSAN (*teasingly*): No, say no, Norma.

MRS. DALE: Mr. Rattigan is handsome and manly.

NORMA: That he is. But he is a big baby. I have seen him rake his sister over the coals, and then beg her forgiveness, crying.

FRANCIS (*smiling*): Crying?

NORMA: Well—that's how I feel about it. I can't bear to see a man crying. That just finishes me.

ERNEST: Let's hope Mr. Rattigan doesn't exploit that weakness.

(*Francis laughs as he takes a sip from his glass.*)

NORMA: Make fun of it if you wish . . . But you cry yourself sometimes.

ERNEST: I do? (*Laughs loudly.*)

NORMA: Oh, I remember last Christmas Eve very well. You thought we two were so poor and lonely. We both sat here on the sofa and cried.

ERNEST (*is overcome by a distress which he tries to conceal*): You cried, Norma—and I tried to comfort you.

NORMA: And the limousine—have you forgotten that?

ERNEST (*grasps the word, like a straw for a drowning man*): Ah, yes, the limousine—that was a frightful catastrophe. Francis, I've quite forgotten to offer you a new cigar.

NORMA (*surprised*): A catastrophe?

FRANCIS (*empties his glass and gets to his feet*): No thanks, I won't smoke any more.

SUSAN (*gets up*): Well, now we'll be leaving, too. (*Goes out into the hallway.*)

MRS. DALE (*gets up*): Goodbye, little Norma. And let's see you again soon. (*Kisses her on the cheek and goes out.*)

(*Ernest accompanies the ladies out into the hall, closes the door.*)

FRANCIS: Mrs. McIntyre—I'm so very fond of both of you. You mustn't be angry at me, will you promise?

NORMA: Yes, in advance, Mr. McLean. What have I done now that's wrong?

FRANCIS: Can you ask, can you really ask seriously about that?

NORMA: Yes—what in heaven's name are you alluding to?

FRANCIS: I'm alluding to what you said about last Christmas Eve.

NORMA: Oh poof, is that all? I thought it was some frightful crime.

FRANCIS: My dear Mrs. McIntyre. You think it is only an innocent trifle. But it hurt your husband deeply. I'm the first to admit that women are the beautiful sex; I will not contradict anyone who calls them the weaker sex. But men are the sensitive sex.

NORMA: This mimosa-like sensitivity—no, I just don't understand it.

FRANCIS: That is what I am afraid of. So much the more reason to be considerate. I mean that—I mean it seriously. We all have, locked within our inmost selves, memories so intimate that it would be sacrilege to draw aside the veil that conceals them. And as you certainly know better than I—it would be hard to find a more sensitive man than he.

NORMA: It is a regular disease. You offend him without intending to, without even knowing it. By trifles that no one—

SUSAN (*tears the door open and enters, dressed in her evening wrap*): Goodbye, Norma. (*Holds out her hand.*) I'll call you tomorrow.

NORMA: Goodbye, Sue. Yes, about noon.

SUSAN: Fine. (*Turns to Francis.*)

FRANCIS: No, I'm leaving, too. Goodbye, Mrs. McIntyre.

NORMA (*takes his extended hand*): Is there such a hurry?

FRANCIS: Yes, I have a long trip home, all the way to Flushing. Good night.

NORMA: Good night, Mr. McLean.

(*Francis nods and smiles to her, exits after Susan. Norma*

17

opens the door in the rear wall, goes over to the table on the right, puts the glasses and the ashtray on the whiskey tray and carries it into the other room, but leaves the coffee things. Comes back and stops before the mirror in the chiffoniere. When the outside door is heard to close, she turns around, though not immediately. Ernest enters, with a gloomy expression. Sits down in an easy chair by the table.)

NORMA (*over to him with arms extended*): Don't I get a kiss?

ERNEST: Don't touch me.

NORMA: What have I done now?

(*Ernest doesn't answer.*)

NORMA: Why don't you answer when I ask you? . . . If there is anything that makes you angry, please tell me about it . . . Why won't you talk to me?

(*Ernest breathes heavily, but is silent.*)

NORMA (*throws herself on the sofa and starts sobbing. But without hope of its having any effect, she sits up and puts her hands on the table*): Ernest—it's my birthday today. (*Ernest is silent as before.*)

NORMA: I'm so happy about the watch. It's the nicest gift you have ever given me. (*Looks at it with a smile of delight.*)

ERNEST (*is softened, but has difficulty restraining himself*): How could you do it, Norma—in front of everybody?

NORMA: What? What did I do? I haven't the faintest notion of what you mean.

ERNEST: "But you cry yourself sometimes"—just saying words like that in front of others.

NORMA: I never dreamed it would hurt you.

ERNEST (*shakes his head*): No, of course . . . And then when it isn't even true.

NORMA: You surely haven't forgotten it, Ernest?

ERNEST: "Sometimes" isn't the same thing as "once." No, I haven't forgotten last Christmas Eve. We two were alone here, alone in the whole city, we thought. The gifts we ex-

18

changed were a cheap luncheon cloth and a box of cigars. Neither of us dared be the first to produce so poor a gift. Then, when you mentioned the limousine, this promise I made you so many years ago, which you had looked forward to having fulfilled just as I did to fulfilling it—then I fell to my knees a moment under the burden of poverty . . . And now, tonight, tonight you—

NORMA: I see now that it wasn't nice of me. I'm very sorry about it.

ERNEST: What good does that do? If only Francis hadn't been present—

NORMA: I can assure you that Francis didn't even notice it.

ERNEST: You are blind, Norma. Didn't you see that he got up solely because it was embarrassing for him to listen to it?

NORMA (*gets up and walks over to him*): I have waited so impatiently to be alone with you this evening. Now you must forgive me, Ernest. I'll never forget that three weeks after this sad Christmas Eve you laid five hundred dollars on the table and sent me to Florida. That was so lovely of you. Now kiss me. (*Kisses him.*)

ERNEST: Have you been satisfied with the day?

NORMA: It is the nicest birthday I ever had.

ERNEST (*caresses her*): That's good, little one. (*Starts pacing back and forth.*)

(*Norma sits down in the armchair. Short silence.*)

NORMA: Did you see the splendid bracelet Susan got today?

ERNEST: Yes . . . It was very elegant and very tasteless. A gift of course?

NORMA: Yes, from Mr. Wallace. It cost six hundred dollars.

ERNEST: How do you know that?

NORMA: She said so. (*With a sigh.*) Well, some people are lucky.

(*Ernest looks at her, starts pacing again.*)

NORMA: Ernest!

ERNEST: Yes.

19

NORMA: Do you think Susan is planning to get married?

ERNEST: Don't know.

NORMA: Do you think there is anything between them, between her and Mr. Wallace?

ERNEST: Between them?

NORMA: I mean—anything really intimate—

ERNEST: I guess there's so much between them that sometimes there isn't anything between them.

NORMA (*laughs*): Shame, Ernest! You're being wicked.

ERNEST: I thought that was what you were asking about. (*Over to the flower table.*) Tell me instead where you got all these flowers. I haven't had time to look at them . . . The red roses, where do they come from?

NORMA: Aunt Cecily.

ERNEST: And the lilacs?

NORMA (*gets up and goes over to him*): Mr. and Mrs. Ives.

ERNEST: They are lovely. The yellow roses, are they from Miss Bell?

NORMA: No, Dr. Briscoe, wasn't that nice of him? I like him so much.

ERNEST: So do I. And the little bunch of violets?

NORMA: Louise. And the calla lily is from Miss Bell.

ERNEST: So she sent that . . . But who sent the basket of Italian anemones?

NORMA: Aunt Cecily.

ERNEST: Aunt Cecily! Did she send both a bouquet and a basket? You said the dark red roses were from her.

NORMA: No, I never said that.

ERNEST: Well, who are they from?

NORMA: I don't know. There was no card.

ERNEST: Anonymous, then.

NORMA: Maybe so. Maybe they forgot to include the card in the flower shop.

(*Ernest walks silently over to the armchair and sits down.*)

NORMA: Ernest, will you tell me something?

ERNEST: What?

NORMA: This evening, when I mentioned the limousine, and you said that it had been a "frightful catastrophe," what did you mean?

ERNEST: Heavens, don't you understand such a simple thing? I chose a word at random, a word that would be strong enough to explain my tears. That was all . . . Please sit down, Norma. I want to talk to you.

NORMA: Yes, if you will kiss me.

ERNEST: Sit down on the sofa here.

NORMA: Yes, of course. You frighten me. What do you want? (*Goes over to the sofa and sits down.*)

ERNEST (*after a moment's silence*): Norma—will you fulfill a serious wish of mine?

NORMA: What is it?

ERNEST: Will you agree to dissolve our marriage?

NORMA (*cries out*): Ernest—. (*Jumps up and starts towards him.*)

ERNEST (*gets up immediately*): Sit down. Sit down, while I talk to you. (*Remains standing until she has sat down.*) (*Norma leans forward on the table and starts crying.*)

ERNEST: It won't do you any good to cry. It has no effect on me any more. The only thing that has any effect on me now is to see that you are willing to let me live in peace. If you start crying, I'll get up and leave.

NORMA: No, you mustn't leave me. You mustn't leave me . . . I won't cry. (*Dries her eyes.*)

ERNEST: It is nineteen days since you came back home from Florida. During these nineteen days I have been puzzling my head about it night and day. This is not a momentary mood. It is the result of the only idea I have been able to formulate in a hell of nineteen days and nineteen nights.

NORMA: Oh God in heaven! What have I done to you,

21

Ernest? I don't know what to do. (*Without expression.*) I
don't know anything—not anything.—

ERNEST: You don't love me any more, Norma.

NORMA: Don't I love you? You are the only, only man on
earth that I do love.

ERNEST: You can't judge that.

NORMA: Can't I judge whether I love you? Who else can
judge it?

ERNEST: I can. Only I can judge it. You can plead such and
such about your feelings, but only I can judge whether your
plea is valid or not. Solomon's judgment was a wise judgment because he let the child make the decision. What good
do all your assurances do me—when I feel that your attitude, your actions, your whole relationship to me is dic-
tated by quite different motives than any that can be
reconciled with my conception of love. You don't love me,
Norma. And therefore—

NORMA: And you, do you love me?

ERNEST: You will have to answer that question yourself.

NORMA: Yes, I know. That is the reason you ask me for
a divorce. If you loved me, you would not chase me away.
You know that I have no one to turn to. No one in the
whole world.

ERNEST: If it is your conviction, Norma, that I don't love
you, then there is twice as much reason for us to part. When
things have reached such a pass that two people are con-
vinced they don't love each other, do *you* believe in a happy
continuation of their marriage? I don't.

NORMA: We have been married for nine years. You can't
expect that the first flames of love should last through an
entire marriage. I don't think there are any marriages—

ERNEST: That is not what I mean. If love were a duty, one
could extend its sources indefinitely. But as long as you
loved me, you tied invisible bonds between your actions
and my wishes. Wishes that you did not know, but which

your instincts taught you. And now—now—. (*He falls silent, and holds his hands before his eyes.*)

NORMA: I'll be so good to you, Ernest.

ERNEST: No, you won't. Because you can't. But you can do something else. You must realize that I have studied the change in you since your return from Florida. I have studied it with chemical precision, and analyzed it atom by atom. You must realize this.

NORMA: Change—I don't understand you, I don't understand what you mean.

(*Ernest is silent.*)

NORMA: You are wrong, Ernest. I am not changed . . . I don't think I have ever loved you as much as I have since I came home. I looked forward every day I was gone to getting back home to you again. Mr. and Miss Rattigan called me "the young bride" and did nothing but tease me all day. And the evening I got home—didn't you notice how happy I was?

ERNEST: Yes, I noticed everything. I noticed that your happiness had no connection with me. You were farther away, many times farther away from me that evening than at any time while you were in Florida. Do you remember that evening yourself? You got your family and your friends up here and kept them until two o'clock. When they left and I wanted to go to bed, you said that I could just go to sleep, and then you used more than an hour and a half on your undressing. When you finally did come in, there was a hard expression on your face when you saw that I was awake. As soon as you had gone to bed, you declared, without any advances on my part, that you were so terribly tired. This unnecessary, preventive insult hurt me deeply, and I hated it. Yet that night it was two months since we had seen each other.

NORMA: Now you are too unreasonable. Can you blame me for being tired after the long, wearisome journey?

ERNEST: You were so tired that every time one of the guests got up to leave, you begged him to stay another half hour. And what do you say about the following evenings? From the time I get home from the lab, you are in a bad humor if we are alone, merry if we are several together. And you go to bed with the same shameless formula about your always being tired.

NORMA: I *have* been terribly tired these weeks since I got home—tired and dizzy. You know that. But now it'll soon go away. I think it's the change of air.

ERNEST: Yes, I think so too. The sudden change of air from Florida.

NORMA: Exactly.

ERNEST: Or maybe the flying?

NORMA: No, the flying doesn't hurt me. Quite the opposite. I am never in such fine condition as when I just get out of the airplane.

ERNEST: I have noticed that. On the other hand, I have also noticed that flying has a very dulling effect on your memory.

NORMA: What kind of a remark is that?

ERNEST: You told me on the telephone today that you had flown to Boston. This evening you said it was Washington.

NORMA: It was Washington. You misunderstood me on the telephone. You admitted yourself this evening that you remembered wrong.

ERNEST: I don't unmask my wife's lies in company. You first told Mr. McLean that you hadn't flown at all today. Until I called your attention to it.

NORMA: Oh,—I was just absentminded for a moment.

ERNEST: You also told me this evening that the dark red roses were from your aunt. Half a minute later you had to admit that they were anonymous.

NORMA: Good lord! Don't you ever remember something wrongly? If a person had to take every detail so solemnly, life wouldn't be worth living.

ERNEST (*gets up and paces back and forth on the floor*): Why can't you keep your secrets secret from me? That is what irritates me. This technical helplessness. To forget the little things, which then reveal the larger ones. When you want to conceal from me that Mr. Rattigan sends you flowers, why in heaven's name can't you see to it that your aunts stick to the flowers they originally selected? When you go downtown in the morning to meet him, why in the name of God can't you remember throughout the day that Thursday was Boston and that Washington doesn't come before Monday?

NORMA: There, you let the cat out of the bag. Finally. You're jealous. (*Gets up.*)

ERNEST: Do you think so?

NORMA: Yes, now I know it. That is why you are acting like this toward me.

ERNEST (*with stronger emphasis*): Do you think so?

NORMA (*more uncertainly*): Yes—if you love me.

ERNEST: If I love you, you say. That was an unconscious admission, wasn't it?

NORMA: It was no admission. Mr. Rattigan is a good friend and I am very fond of him. But I don't love him and I never will. You are angry because I like him. I have no reason not to do so. He has been unusually kind to me. But whenever a man shows me kindness, you find something suspicious in it. You can't expect that nobody else but you will like a young and pretty woman just because you are married to her. You are jealous, but you don't dare admit it. And why? Because your reason tells you that you have no basis for it.

ERNEST: Hasn't it dawned on you after we have been married for nine years how different in their nature your and my love are? In the short period we lived together happily and harmoniously, it sometimes happened that the conscience of hope stirred in both of us. And you asked yourself: "Will he ever love another woman?" My joy was

25

prouder: "Will she ever stop loving me?" I asked. No, I am not jealous, Norma. I haven't the shadow of a desire to investigate whether you love another man. The only thing that interests me is this: your love for me has cooled.

NORMA: That isn't right, Ernest. You must be blind if you can't see how much I love you.

ERNEST: I won't be fooled, Norma. I tell you so in advance. If you came to me now and said that it no longer suited you to carry on our life together, you wouldn't need to make any explanations, or give any reasons. I would go my own way quietly without bitterness or resentment . . . But I won't be fooled.

NORMA: In reality you don't love me at all.

ERNEST: Yes, I know you have trouble understanding such an assurance, which is so entirely contrary to your own nature. But have I ever given you the faintest grounds for even the slightest suspicion? You have. More than faint grounds. I have no decisive proofs against you. But I am not mistaken. My instinct has a thousand eyes, and they all see the same thing. You want to fool me, Norma. But now I beg you: don't let it go that far. Let us prevent it before it is too late. Let us part.

NORMA (*over to him with outstretched arms*): Ernest—

ERNEST: No, no. I want a decision on this matter.

NORMA (*throws herself weeping into the armchair*): What does it help what I say, when you suspect my every word in advance? (*Conceals her face in her hands.*)
(*Ernest leans against the bookcase and looks out into the distance a long time. Then he slowly walks over to Norma and strokes her hair with his hand. Norma caresses his legs feverishly and whispers gasping words that are not heard.*)

CURTAIN

ACT II

Same room. Next day.

(*Norma, Susan, and Mrs. Dale sitting by the table right.*)

NORMA (*offering chocolates*): Have some, mother.

MRS. DALE: Thanks.

NORMA: Chocolates, Susan.

SUSAN: No, they're fattening . . . I'm leaving now anyway. It's two o'clock.

NORMA: Oh, you could wait a moment. Ernest said he would call at two o'clock. Then we'll go together. Just a couple of minutes.

SUSAN: I know your "couple of minutes." I'll wait until two-thirty and not a moment longer.

NORMA: By two-thirty I'll be downtown. Say, there is something I would like to ask you two to do.

MRS. DALE: Us? What is it, little Norma?

NORMA: I'm going to fly with Mr. Rattigan, and I'm going to meet him at 3:45—

SUSAN: Fly two days running?

NORMA: Yes, but Ernest won't believe it—

SUSAN: I can't blame him for that.

NORMA: What's so strange about that? Mr. Rattigan does what he likes.

SUSAN: Yes, it looks that way.

NORMA: How are the Cliffords doing, Susan? Well, it doesn't matter. Ernest has gotten so ridiculously jealous lately. I had a long scene with him yesterday evening, after you had left. So I have to be careful—

MRS. DALE: Yes, for God's sake, be careful.

(*Susan smiles maliciously.*)

NORMA: I don't dare tell him I'm flying today. It pains me to tell him a lie. And it's just to spare him unpleasantness that I do it. It's for his own sake.

MRS. DALE: Yes, I know men, I assure you. You should preferably tell him you have stopped flying with Mr. Rattigan.

SUSAN: Nonsense, mother. That will only confirm his suspicion.

NORMA: No, I won't do that. But I only tell him every third or fourth time. I'm expecting his call any moment, and I have to tell him I've been invited to tea with you at Mrs. Beauchamp's.

SUSAN: Why with us? No, I won't do that.

NORMA: You could do that much for me. Haven't I done you similar favors many times, Susan? Yes, mother, you know how strict father could be with her.

MRS. DALE: Yes, you are right about that. And with you, too.

NORMA: You two have to have been with me. If he gets suspicious, it's so easy just to refer to you.

SUSAN: And then he calls up Mrs. Beauchamp while we are

28

there—or rather, while we are not there—and finds out that she has never invited us to tea.

NORMA: Of course I won't tell him until later. I'll tell him that she called right after I put the receiver down.

SUSAN: And tomorrow he will call her up and ask if she remembers that you take lemon with your tea and not cream.

NORMA: No, Ernest won't do that. He doesn't spy. He is too proud for that.

SUSAN: This is unwise of you, Norma. You are a regular bungler. Just tell him straight out that we have been at a dog show at the Waldorf Astoria. Or that you have gone with me to pick out a couple of dresses at Stern Brothers. In the middle of the day. That would work out fine.

NORMA: No, Mrs. Beauchamp is necessary. You don't know Ernest. There is no limit to his suspiciousness of me. He suspects all three of us of a secret plot against him.

MRS. DALE: The three of us? I've never heard the like of it!

NORMA (*listening*): Sh! . . . That's impossible! He's coming home now! Yes, it is Ernest. (*Looks at her watch and gets up.*) You mustn't fail me. I won't get away from home if we don't say it.

ERNEST (*enters from the rear*): Hello. (*Greets Mrs. Dale and Susan.*)

NORMA: How does it happen that you came home now?

ERNEST: Oh, I'm going to work with some drawings. I have to compare them with others that I have here at home.

NORMA: Then you're leaving right away again?

ERNEST: No, I'm working with them here at home. But now I'm going to take a couple of hours off. You aren't going out during these next two hours are you?

SUSAN (*gets up*): No, Norma is staying home. But we're leaving.

MRS. DALE: Oh, but you can't do that, Susan. The last time

we were at Mrs. Beauchamp's Norma couldn't come, either. And now she's expecting the three of us and is looking forward to seeing us.

ERNEST (*to Norma*): Are you going to Mrs. Beauchamp's? I didn't know that.

NORMA: Yes, I had promised her to have tea at her place today.

ERNEST: But of course you'll go. Did she call you today?

NORMA: Yes, this morning right after you had left. (*Suspiciously eager.*) But of course, if you would rather have me stay home—

ERNEST: No, no. I guess I need all my time. And whatever you promise you should keep. (*Looks at her.*) It's really almost novel for me to see you on a weekday, in daylight. (*With a faint smile.*) Novel and rather strange.

NORMA: I don't feel that when one has promised something—

ERNEST: No, you're quite right. One should do the very opposite: one should keep *more* than one has promised. I haven't promised to have tea at Mrs. Beauchamp's. But now I will. I'll go with you. (*Embarrassed silence.*)

NORMA: Yes, but—Ernest, you can't invite yourself.

ERNEST: Yes, by God. To such good friends. It just didn't occur to her that I would have time to come along. In the middle of the day. Otherwise she would have asked me, too. She'll be glad to see me.

MRS. DALE: Mrs. Beauchamp is very formal. That's what I like about her. And she has invited us to a *ladies'* tea. You just can't act like that. Then I won't go at all.

SUSAN: Is it a ladies' tea—heaven forbid! You didn't tell me that, mother. Then I'll withdraw too.

NORMA: Then, Susan, we'll go in and tell her we can't come . . . And we'll drop in for a while at the dog show. I just *have* to see that.

ERNEST: Can't come? No, you just can't act like that. Of course we'll all go. And now I'll call Mrs. Beauchamp and let her know that I'm coming. (*Goes to the door left.*)

NORMA (*runs in front of him*): No, Ernest, no. You mustn't do that.

ERNEST: What's that? I *mustn't* do it? Can't I call Mrs. Beauchamp?

NORMA: No, Ernest, you must understand. If we all go, *I* would much rather talk to her and just tell her that I'm taking my husband with me—rather than have you call her. Let *me* call.

ERNEST: As you wish.

NORMA: Come, Susan. (*They exit through the door left.*) (*Ernest proceeds to pace up and down the floor, silent and intent.*)

MRS. DALE: You mustn't misunderstand me, Ernest. But when I talked to Mrs. Beauchamp on the telephone this morning, she specially pointed out that it was a ladies' tea. And she is so terribly formal. It's the only thing I don't like about her.

ERNEST: I don't misunderstand you . . . I understand you much better than you think.

MRS. DALE (*kindly*): Didn't I know it, you were just teasing us. (*Gets up from the sofa.*) But then I'll go out and tell Norma that she won't need to call.

ERNEST: No, I want Norma to call.

(*Mrs. Dale sits down on the sofa again, silent but uneasy.*)

ERNEST: So you have joined this plot of lies, too, Lillian Dale?

MRS. DALE: Are you addressing *me* in that way? I won't stand for it.

ERNEST: You're going to have to stand for it. I'm only accusing you of something you can't deny. You have said that Mrs. Beauchamp invited you and my wife for tea today. That is a lie. Mrs. Beauchamp has been in Chicago for three days and will stay there for five days more. Her sister called me today to ask if Norma had liked the birthday gift that Mrs. Beauchamp had asked her to pick out.

MRS. DALE (*loftily to conceal her embarrassment*): You are jealous.—That's ridiculous.

ERNEST: Are you saying that as an excuse for your lie?

MRS. DALE: I only say it to show you how you are mistreating your wife. Norma was the liveliest child in New York before she was married. Now she goes around with a sad face and has no real happiness any more. You have frightened and plagued her so long that she doesn't feel safe anywhere. You have suspected her without reason until she no longer dares to tell you the innocent truth and has to have her mother and sister help conceal it. If I were in her place, I would have asked for a divorce a long time ago.

ERNEST: And gotten it . . . But I would be willing to grant Norma a better defense. You know that what you are saying about "frightening" and "suspecting" her is just empty talk. It's something you resort to because I've caught you red-handed. And I wouldn't have suspected Norma today either, if I hadn't learned that you are the one that taught her to lie.

(*Mrs. Dale gets up, walks rapidly across the floor towards the door left, and wants to leave.*)

ERNEST (*blocks the door*): Where are you going?

MRS. DALE: I want to leave. Do you think I will stay in the same room with a man who insults me?

ERNEST: You're not leaving until Norma comes back.

(*Mrs. Dale goes towards the door in the rear.*)

ERNEST (*blocks the door to her*): You'll have to stay here for the time being.

(*Mrs. Dale again hurries to the door left.*)

ERNEST (*blocks the door*): It is of no use your trying to get out. I want to hear Norma's explanation, without your interference. Even if I should have to hold you back forcibly.

MRS. DALE (*calling*): Norma, Norma, your husband is laying hands on me.

ERNEST: Why do you lie? I'm not touching you.

MRS. DALE: Norma!

ERNEST: It's no use your calling. Norma and Susan can't come back in before they have consulted on what to say. It takes a little time.

(*Mrs. Dale goes to a chair, where she sits down, with her back to Ernest.*)

ERNEST (*closer to her*): I hate you, Lillian Dale.

MRS. DALE: Do you think it comes as a surprise to me? I can very well tell you what the reason is. You are jealous of me too. You can't bear it that Norma is as fond of me as she is.

ERNEST: I hate you, and I cannot forgive you. I can't forgive you that you have warped and corrupted Norma's character from childhood. I said that you had taught her to lie. It is frightful to say such harsh words to her mother, or to any human being. Even so it is only a small part of my accusation. I'll do you all the justice you are entitled to. Today is really the first time I have caught you in an out-and-out lie. If I should judge only by this, I could judge you rather mildly. But you have cultivated everything that is weak and untrustworthy in Norma's character. She had an inclination to exaggerate, and you were amused by her exaggerations. And when she discovered that she could amuse you doubly by exaggerating doubly—what was the result? The result was that no one who knows her believes a word she says. I understand much better than you yourself where the real basis for this frailty is to be found. And I would be glad to advance it as an extenuation for you if it were not at the same time a testimonial to your frightening lack of responsibility. You lived in an unhappy marriage. And the greatest

33

misfortune was that your husband was at the same time honest and weak of character. When he scolded Norma for her dishonesty, you found delight in irritating him by taking her side. The more severely he chastised this weakness, the more certain was her protection from you. That is why she came to be closer to you than to him. That is the source of her filial affection. But some day she will have her eyes opened—

MRS. DALE: Do you think I have ever been in doubt as to who was responsible for the small love Norma has shown me since she was married? It's very pretty now, isn't it, to sow dissension between mother and child! Very pretty and noble!

ERNEST: If anyone on this earth has tried to sow dissension between two people, that person is you. From the day I had my first great disappointment with my patents, you used your whole influence to wean Norma's heart away from me. You daily encouraged her burning need of luxury. And instead of Norma and me fighting poverty together, I often had to fight both of them alone.

MRS. DALE: It sounds very nice. But in my language it only says that you proved unable to support your wife in a respectable way.

(*Ernest smiles faintly, after which his face turns hard again, but he says nothing. Susan and Norma enter from the left.*)

SUSAN (*breathlessly*): Just imagine, mother—Ernest. Somebody or other has been playing tricks on us over the telephone. (*Walks around among the others as she is speaking.*) Mrs. Beauchamp isn't in town at all. And somebody actually must have pretended to be Mrs. Beauchamp and tried to fool us. What luck that we called! But the nerve of it! What do you say about the nerve of someone who would *lie* like that on the telephone. Anyway it's funny that neither you nor Norma—not even you, Norma—could tell it from the

34

voice. As far as that goes the same thing exactly happened to me the other day. Elsie Clifford called up and talked a long time with me, and then it wasn't her at all. But imagine our being invited to Mrs. Beauchamp's—and then Mrs. Beauchamp is in Chicago!

ERNEST: Yes, she's been there for three days, and she'll be staying for five more.

(*Mrs. Dale disappears into the hall.*)

SUSAN (*stops dead in her tracks from surprise*): You know it? . . . That's exactly what the servant answered.

ERNEST: Yes, Mrs. Allan called me this morning.

SUSAN: You knew that she had left. And still you let us call. You stand here and put on an act and pretend that you want to go with us. That's dirty!

ERNEST: You can save yourself all this pretense. You are red in the face with shame for your part in this game. Shame which all your nerve can't conceal.

SUSAN: My part! Heaven help us! I haven't gotten any telephone invitation to Mrs. Beauchamp's, if that is what you mean. But I don't suppose you are accusing your wife and your mother-in-law of lying?

ERNEST: Yes, and my sister-in-law, too. Your mother admitted it while you were out.

MRS. DALE (*sticks her head through the door, with her wraps on*): Goodbye, Norma.

(*Norma follows her into the hall.*)

SUSAN: Now I'll tell you one thing, Ernest McIntyre. It's not hard to fool sharper men than you are. But you can't fool me. Now I have seen through you. You are ridiculously, fantastically, madly jealous. You thought Norma was going down to see Mr. Rattigan today. And so you bribed some female or other to call us to see if she would refuse the invitation. That is why you came home in the middle of your working day. But you reckoned wrong. I have seen

35

through you, you can bet your life on that. I have seen through you. (*Rushes out and slams the door behind her.*) (*Ernest goes over to a chair, pulls it away from the table, but decides not to sit down, and puts the chair down with a bang. Over to the rear door, but decides not to enter it, and closes it without a sound. Paces the floor for a while. Norma enters from the left, pale and depressed, quietly goes over to the sofa, lies down, and starts crying.*)

ERNEST: Why are you crying, Norma?

(*Norma does not answer, but only sobs harder.*)

ERNEST: Why are you crying, I asked.

NORMA (*sits up, takes a handkerchief out of her purse on the table, and dries her eyes*): What have you done to mother, Ernest? She said that she would never set foot in my house again while you were there. What have you done to her?

ERNEST: If that is all that troubles you, I can comfort you by reminding you that your mother says that on the average four times a year. But now I think you should pull yourself together, fix yourself up, and go where you were planning to go when I came home. It's twenty minutes to three, and Mr. Rattigan must be longing for you.

NORMA: Why are you so mean to me? It is all your own fault. You know that this man means nothing to me. But you have made me so frightened that I don't even dare tell you that I have met him on the street, much less that I have been flying with him two days in a row—

ERNEST: Yes, I know that explanation. Your mother gave me exactly the same lecture. It is impossible to mistake it. It is a standing explanation of all women who have been caught in infidelity.

NORMA: I have never been unfaithful to you, and if I had any wish for it, I would get a divorce from you first. But when you suspect me all the time, I have to buy a little peace for you and me by telling you a lie. You yourself have forced this dishonesty between us.

ERNEST: You see how much peace your method brings into our home. (*Sits down.*) No, Norma. You mustn't think it is your stratagem today that convinces me of your infidelity. That causes me hardly any sorrow. Anger yes, but not sorrow. I'm not satisfied with this shell. I crack it in order to get in to the kernel of these events. And what do I see then? If you loved me, Norma, if your finest feelings were not dulled, you would think in this way: "I have noticed that my husband is unhappy if I am mentioned in connection with Mr. Rattigan. I can't quite make him understand how natural my association with this man is. I won't cause him any unhappiness. I will break my association with Mr. Rattigan." You would not have waited for me to express my displeasure *if* you loved me. And *after* I expressed it, you would even less have kept up this kind of behavior.

NORMA: What are you asking me to do? Tell me straight out. It was agreed between Mr. Rattigan and me yesterday that we should fly again today. Then came this scene last night which made me afraid to tell you about it. I couldn't make myself ridiculous by calling off the appointment.

ERNEST: Only a woman who does not love her husband would talk like that.

NORMA: One who is not her husband's slave.

ERNEST (*loses his patience, gets up*): Why do you go on flying with Mr. Rattigan when you see that I don't approve of it?

NORMA: You know that flying is my only remaining pleasure on earth. Are you going to take away that one, too? I could say that if you loved me, you too would think differently. You would think: "I have promised her that she could have nice clothes, go to Europe, have her own country estate, her own car, her own yacht, and I haven't been able to give her any of this. If I now take this last pleasure away from her, she will see that I don't love her any more."

ERNEST (*giving up*): Well, Norma—then I don't love you any more.

NORMA: Don't you think I've seen it for a long time?

ERNEST: You have seen it for a long time. So you *have* thought it over. I hope that will make it easier for you to accept my declaration.

NORMA: What do you mean?

ERNEST: I mean it ought to be enough to reach my goal: a divorce.

NORMA: It's not true, Ernest, that you don't love me any more. I know it isn't true. And I'll be so good, so good to you . . . I'll stop flying with Mr. Rattigan, if you wish. Do you hear, I'll stop.

ERNEST: "I'll stop!" You have been married to me for nine years, and still you don't have the key to my mind. You talk as if the happiness of two people were a dictate which one person gives and the other follows.

NORMA (*repeats monotonously*): I'll be so good, so good to you.

ERNEST: You have never been good to me.

NORMA (*gets up*): Those were poor thanks, Ernest.

ERNEST: Poorest for me, who values them according to their deserts.

NORMA: I have never thought of making my marriage into a business proposition. One's love doesn't ask if it is deserved or not. I would like to see any woman of my class who would have shared nine years of poverty as I have done.

ERNEST: I would like to see any woman who has let me know about that poverty oftener than you have.

NORMA: And haven't I taken care of my home without a maid all these years?

ERNEST: Oh, don't let's bicker about trifles!

NORMA: Trifles! Everything *I* do is trifles.

ERNEST: No, these are trifles because your housekeeping has only caused me unpleasantness, but there are things in your character that have caused me sorrow and despair.

NORMA: Have you always thought that my housekeeping caused you unpleasantness? Even when you saw me darning your socks in the evening? Even though I hated darning socks.

ERNEST: You let me know that you hated it. This was the reason I preferred to use them with the holes. It never occurred to you to look. If you had been a good housekeeper, Norma, you would have saved me many a bitter moment. On Friday evenings I often sent a kindly thought to our Negro woman—at your expense. It was about the only evening in the week I didn't have to make my bed in the evening or wash the dishes from the day before. You always put your comfort first and my work second. No matter how important it was or how busy I was. You got up at noon and read in bed until late in the night, even though you knew that I thought best in bed and that the light disturbed me. But all this is trifling compared with the wedge that the last few weeks have driven into our marriage.

NORMA: Now you are being unjust. Don't I always put out the light when you ask me to?

ERNEST: No, you say you will do it in just a couple of minutes. And a couple of minutes for you means anything from an hour and a half, to three hours, or never . . . Who's out in the hall?

NORMA: It's Kate.

ERNEST: That's right, it's Friday.

NORMA (*after a moment's thought*): If I now promise you that I will stop flying—you know it's my greatest joy—if I now give up my greatest joy, can't we then forget all the

39

ugly and unpleasant things that have sneaked in between us?

ERNEST: Just the fact that you ask it in this way is enough to kill my last hope, if it existed. This lack of sensitivity, connecting your "greatest joy" with all that has caused my deepest torment—at the same moment as you try to bring about a reconciliation. More than that—you want to make these two opposites into a basis for reconciliation.

NORMA: Was that wrong too? I must ask you to excuse me, Ernest. I thought that when you saw what a sacrifice I would make, you would also realize how much I loved you.

ERNEST: No, Norma. I see that it is an attempt to freshen up feelings that have cooled. And I don't believe in warmed-over dishes of any kind, whether in marriage or in the kitchen. Try to forget, you say. A person only forgets what is unimportant. You never forget a sharp point that has touched your heart. Whether the point is that of a dagger or of a despair. We can *say* that we forget, just to comfort the one who caused the pain. But we don't do it just the same.

NORMA (*sits down on a chair by the table*): You give *me* the blame for everything that has gone wrong in our marriage. Isn't it curious that nothing of all this would have given you any basis for accusation if *poverty* hadn't been waiting for me on the threshold of our marriage and never let go its hold on me? You knew when we were married that I was not suited for domestic duties. If you had given me a maid, I would never have had to listen to your bitter words about the housekeeping. And this blessed flying! If I had had the money to join a flying club, or even to do some ordinary flying as a passenger on one of the airlines—don't you think I would have done so the moment I noticed that I could save myself unpleasantness and scenes by rejecting Edward Rattigan's offers?

40

ERNEST: This is what you call sharing nine years of poverty with me!

NORMA: Aren't you tired of never granting yourself any pleasures? *I* am.

ERNEST: I will be glad to buy you a membership card in a flying club as soon as I can afford to bestow so expensive a pleasure on you. But if I should want to get hold of you in a hurry during flying hours, I would be likely to find you in Mr. Rattigan's rooms. That is what I want to avoid.

NORMA: Then I'll give you a much better piece of advice. Just buy a leash for me, as short as you think is necessary, and keep me on it. That is the only way you can be sure of me.

ERNEST: You are quite right. It is the only way I can be sure of you. And for that reason I have proposed the only solution that will satisfy me: let's get divorced. When it has reached a point where I cannot with full confidence grant you all the freedom you might wish in your marriage, then I can no longer be married to you. I beg you to remember that I have not for a moment tried to restrain your movements. I have asked you for a divorce, but have not with one word asked you to remove the grounds for my request.

NORMA: I have offered you to remove them.

ERNEST: It is an offer I cannot accept. We have talked long enough about this matter . . . Why do you let Mr. Rattigan wait so long? If you are not in a humor to—"fly," why don't you call him?

NORMA: Do you think he is waiting for me? If one isn't there on the dot, he flies away. He has flown long ago, you may be sure.

ERNEST: Alone—without you!

NORMA: I have never flown alone with Mr. Rattigan. We are always at least five together. Does that make you feel better?

ERNEST: No, neither better nor worse. (*The doorbell rings.*)

NORMA: It's Dr. Briscoe—I know it by the ringing.

ERNEST: Are you expecting him?

NORMA: No.

ERNEST: No, of course. How can I ask? (*Kate, a middle-aged colored woman, knocks on the door left and comes in with a calling card in her hand.*)

NORMA (*takes the card and starts*): Say I am not at home.

KATE: I said the missus was home.

ERNEST: I'm expecting Mr. Rattigan, let him in.

KATE: Yes, sir. (*Exit.*)

NORMA: Are *you* expecting Mr. Rattigan?

ERNEST: No, I saw it on you that it was he.

NORMA (*rushing around*): Oh, God in heaven! You will make a scandal. You will compromise me.

ERNEST: Do I usually do that? You don't need to worry.

NORMA: Oh God! God in heaven!

MR. RATTIGAN (*enters. Tall, squarely-built, about forty years of age, carefully and tastefully dressed. Is holding a bouquet of long-stemmed lilies-of-the-valley in his hand and presents them to Norma*): How do you do, Mrs. McIntyre?

NORMA: How do you do. Thank you. (*Indifferently takes the flowers and goes over to a small table with them.*)

MR. RATTIGAN (*extends his hand to Ernest*): How do you do, Mr. McIntyre?

ERNEST: How do you do, Mr. Rattigan? So happy to see you.

MR. RATTIGAN: I'm happy to see *you*. Mrs. McIntyre and I have been such good friends since we met in Florida, and the lady added to my pleasure by requesting me to visit you once when I thought you might be at home.

ERNEST: I appreciate the kindness you have shown Mrs. McIntyre . . . Please sit down.

MR. RATTIGAN: Thank you. (*Sits down.*)

ERNEST: However, I'm not usually at home at this time.

MR. RATTIGAN (*about to get up again*): Oh, I didn't know that.

ERNEST (*sits down*): No, don't misunderstand me. You *have* found me at home.

MR. RATTIGAN (*smiling*): Well, then I see I have been lucky.

ERNEST: Or *I*, Mr. Rattigan.

(*Norma sits down.*)

ERNEST (*to Norma*): But how was it? Wasn't there an appointment for you to fly with Mr. Rattigan today? (*Looks at his watch.*) Right about this time?

NORMA: Yes, but you know what happened.

ERNEST: I do, but Mr. Rattigan doesn't.

MR. RATTIGAN: It was a good thing that you were prevented from coming, Mrs. McIntyre. For when I got to the hangar, the propellers were out of order.

ERNEST: And so you came here instead. That was nice of you.

MR. RATTIGAN: Mrs. McIntyre told me yesterday that she might be going downtown today, so it was not certain that she could come. So it is really an unexpected pleasure to find Mrs. McIntyre at home too.

(*Ernest sends him a stolen, inquisitive look, says nothing, but nods slightly. The telephone is heard ringing in a room on the other side of the hall. Norma gets up.*)

ERNEST (*beats her to it*): I'll take it. (*Exit through door left.*)

NORMA (*turns on Mr. Rattigan*): Why in the world did you come here without calling me? Run right into my husband's arms. Now you have destroyed my whole life.

MR. RATTIGAN (*gets up*): I'm no less surprised than you— at finding your husband home.

NORMA: You might very well expect to find him home. This is inconsiderate of you.

43

MR. RATTIGAN: No, I couldn't expect that from the wording of the telegram.

NORMA: What telegram?

MR. RATTIGAN: What telegram, you ask? Didn't you send me a telegram to come here at three o'clock?

NORMA: I? . . . Never.

(*Mr. Rattigan pulls a telegram out of his pocket and hands it to her.*)

NORMA (*reading*): "Prevented from coming today. Come home to me exactly at three o'clock." There is no name.

MR. RATTIGAN: No, I admired you for your caution. But I had no suspicion. Our agreement yesterday was that you would come to me today at 2:30. At 1:30 I got this telegram. At 2:50 you hadn't come. It was clear as daylight that the telegram had to be from you.

NORMA: This is incredible . . . It is impossible to understand . . . Who sent this telegram?

MR. RATTIGAN: It's a mystery to me. (*Suddenly a light seems to dawn on him with such compulsive clarity that he shakes his head to keep from revealing it.*)

NORMA: What were you thinking? Do you suspect anyone?

MR. RATTIGAN (*shakes his head*): No.

NORMA: Yes, I saw that you did. (*Suddenly touches her forehead.*) My husband! No, no, no! Never! . . . Was he the one you suspected?

MR. RATTIGAN: Yes, it was.

NORMA: No, it wasn't. You were thinking of someone else. How could he know I was going to meet you?

MR. RATTIGAN: Norma, I'm afraid your husband surpasses both of us in his cleverness. I got that impression the moment I met him. It can't be anyone else.

(*Norma holds the telegram in her hand and reads it through. Ernest enters from the left.*)

NORMA (*turns away and thrusts the telegram quietly into her bosom*): Who was it?

ERNEST: It was from the laboratory . . . I regret that I must ask you to excuse me.

MR. RATTIGAN: Sorry if I have disturbed you. Goodbye, Mr. McIntyre.

ERNEST (*holds out his hand*): By no means. Goodbye.

MR. RATTIGAN: Goodbye, Mrs. McIntyre.

NORMA: Goodbye.

ERNEST (*accompanies him to the door*): Thanks for your visit.

(*Mr. Rattigan is heard answering in the vestibule.*)

ERNEST (*enters again*): You just barely thanked him for the flowers. You didn't thank him at all for the visit. You didn't press him to come again. A man who has shown you so much kindness. Do you know what this means?

NORMA: Why do you keep torturing me like this? You will never make me admit I have been unfaithful to you.

ERNEST: You are impregnable, aren't you?

NORMA: Yes, on that point I am impregnable.

ERNEST: If this is correct, then take out the letter you are hiding in your bosom.

NORMA: It isn't a letter.

ERNEST: Well, telegram then. You sent it to Mr. Rattigan, and it explains his strange visit here today. How, I don't know.

NORMA (*pulls out the telegram*): Then he was right—it was you who sent it. It is a trap which your monstrous jealousy set for him. I would never have believed this about you. Never . . . Here you are.

(*Ernest looks thoughtfully at the telegram.*)

NORMA: I beg your forgiveness, Ernest. I don't believe this about you. I just don't understand you. I don't understand

45

anything. But I beg you to believe me. I swear to you that I haven't sent it.

ERNEST (*hands her the telegram*): I don't need any assurances. You didn't send it. Any more than I did.

NORMA: Can you imagine how this came about?

ERNEST: If I had talked with him as you have done, perhaps I would *know* it . . . I can imagine that he has promised some other woman to meet her today at this time, a week ago maybe, and then just forgot it . . . For one sun a thousand stars are forgotten.

NORMA: You have no reason to make this kind of insinuations.

ERNEST: That is not the crucial point anyway. The crucial point is that when Mr. Rattigan gets an anonymous telegram about meeting a lady in her home, he can't imagine that this lady is anyone but my wife.

NORMA: Nothing is more natural, if only you are willing to see it, when you know that we had agreed to meet today. But what makes you blind is—

ERNEST: My jealousy, yes. It makes me purblind.

NORMA: It is strange that men won't ever admit that they are jealous.

ERNEST: There is nothing strange in that. Men are more reticent than women. And jealousy is the reverse side of love. In it are hidden all the knots, the seams, and the errors of love. But this has nothing to do with the case. I am so little jealous that I wish with all my heart for you to marry Mr. Rattigan.

NORMA: Ha! . . . I could never imagine doing it. (*Stops before the mirror in the chiffoniere.*)

ERNEST (*sits down on a chair by the table*): No, I know that. (*Norma looks at him a little uncertainly.*)

ERNEST: I understand you through and through, Norma. (*Norma sits down in the sofa.*)

ERNEST: There are women who struggle for a shorter or longer period with themselves because they suddenly face the fact that they love two men. Two men whom they can't choose between because they supplement each other; because the one gives them in full measure what the other lacks. I have nothing to say about such a woman except that I happen to be married to one. That I am married to her, and that every fiber in my soul revolts against such a character. It is not enough to me that you choose. That you hesitate to choose offends my pride. No, no, what good does it do for me to try to understand you. To misunderstand everything is to forgive everything.

NORMA: Do you love me, Ernest?

ERNEST: No.

NORMA: What if this "no" has given me a right?

ERNEST: Right to what?

NORMA: To listen to warm and beautiful words that I never heard in my marriage.

ERNEST: That "no" could not give you any right before it was spoken. Until you came home from Florida you possessed my heart whole and undivided. There you failed me. You used the money, which was the very evidence of my love for you, to deceive my trust. While you were in Florida, I sat in the laboratory every single night in order to pay for the cost of your trip.

NORMA: Those five hundred dollars—was that such a big gift in the course of nine years?

ERNEST: No, not big. But fatal.

NORMA: I have not deceived your trust. I have not done anything you could not see. You think everything is much worse than it is. You sat home alone and—don't you remember how prettily you wrote to me once, when you longed so for me: "It's not you, Norma, but the distance that fails me."

ERNEST: Ah yes, distance—there you spoke the word, that

deceptive word. If you had been near enough to me so that I could have exerted my influence, as you did yours, then the game would not have been so unequal. But I was helpless as a child. It was like giving one's opponent a short dagger and keeping a three-foot rapier for oneself! "Now let's fight!" (*Rises and fixes his gaze on her.*) I beg you, Norma, I *beg* you not to oppose my wish any longer. There can't be any life together for us after this.

NORMA (*gets up*): You have no reason, no proofs, nothing but imagination to go on. You can't chase me away like this. You can't take to yourself a woman who gives you the nine best years of her life, who gives you her youth and her beauty, who accepts poverty and self-denial for years—and then chase her out. In a few years I will neither be young nor pretty any more. What will happen to me then? Haven't I been lonely long enough? You haven't the heart to do this, Ernest, I know it.

ERNEST: I'll support you—better than I have done so far. Much, much better. And we are fortunate not to have children. But even if we did have children, you could keep them. All of them. No matter how much I loved them. For this one thing I cannot do any longer: I cannot live with you any longer.

NORMA: You can go—anywhere you wish—and I will follow you.

ERNEST (*is silent a moment, then says firmly*): We shall see. (*Goes into his study.*)
(*Norma goes over to the door on the left, opens it, and lets the door stand ajar. Slowly walks to a chair by the table and hides her face in her hands. A little time passes—then the doorbell rings. Norma looks up, remains seated a few moments, then gets up.*)

KATE (*knocks on the door and enters*): Mr. McLean!

NORMA (*calls out in the hallway*): Hello, Mr. McLean.

FRANCIS (*in the hall*): Hello, Mrs. McIntyre. (*Comes in and shakes her hand.*) How are you?

NORMA: Fine, thank you.

FRANCIS: Isn't Ernest home?

NORMA: Yes, he is in the study.

FRANCIS: Yes, of course. I was sure I would find him at home.

NORMA: How so, Mr. McLean? He doesn't usually come home at this time.

FRANCIS (*surprised*): Hasn't he told you? Has that rascal kept it to himself—sits alone in his study and keeps it to himself? Well, he's certainly going to get a real talking-to. (*Over to the door.*)

ERNEST (*enters*): Hello, Francis!

FRANCIS: Hello. Congratulations, my dear Ernest. A thousand congratulations! . . . But this is the last kindly greeting to you for the next twenty years. Sitting here in your study by yourself and not even telling your wife about the big event!

ERNEST: Well, I came home for that purpose, but there were guests here.

FRANCIS: Oh, bother with the guests. I won't leave, anyway. Don't you see that your wife is on tenterhooks to learn the news? (*Peeks at the books in the bookcase.*)

ERNEST: Norma—I've sold my latest patent.

NORMA (*who has waited a thousand times to hear the sound of these words. Quite involuntarily, as on a well-known signal, she extends her arms*): Ernest—
(*Ernest stands unmoved. Norma's expression darkens, her arms sink slowly, emptily.*)

FRANCIS: All the afternoon papers are full of praise for Ernest. And some of them have his picture—the one uglier than the next. And why don't you mention the sum? One hundred and fifty thousand dollars, Mrs. McIntyre. What do you say to that?

NORMA: One hundred and fifty thousand! (*Goes to a chair and sinks down into it.*)

FRANCIS: I'll go in your study, Ernest, and grab a cigar.

ERNEST: Oh, excuse me—

FRANCIS: No, no, I know very well where they are. (*Exit.*)

NORMA (*about to get up, but stops*): Congratulations, Ernest.

ERNEST: Congratulations, Norma. I gave you that patent on the day I entered it. It is your money.

NORMA (*bursts out crying*): I was much, much richer before it came. (*Silence.*)

ERNEST: Fancy clothes. Trips to Europe. The country estate. The car. The yacht. (*Takes the lilies-of-the-valley and goes over to Norma.*) Fruitful days, and fruitful nights. (*Strikes her in the face with the flowers.*) And now get out of my life. (*Tosses the flowers on the table and goes into the study.*)

(*Norma remains seated in bewilderment. Then a bright smile crosses her face. She gets up and her smile gets warmer and richer. She goes to the doorpost on the left and rings the bell. Kate enters.*)

NORMA: Kate, will you run out on the corner and buy the afternoon papers . . . Every one of them!

KATE: Yes'm. (*Exit.*)

(*Norma goes smiling to the mirror and powders herself.*)

CURTAIN

50

ACT III

Thirteen days later. A spacious room with bay windows on both front corners. Doors on the left and in the rear. Front, a little to the left, an oak desk and two chairs beside it. Aside from this, the room is furnished with white-lacquered bedroom furniture: right rear a bed, to the left a clothes cabinet and a toilet commode with a mirror. In front of the commode a heavy armchair with slats in the back. Front right a daybed. On the table magazines, books, rolls of paper, etc. In the ceiling a large electric chandelier fully lighted.

(*Ernest and Francis sit by the table with whiskey in front of them. Ernest offers cigarettes.*)

FRANCIS: Wouldn't you prefer that I didn't smoke—in your bedroom?

ERNEST: Heavens no—would you rather have a cigar?

FRANCIS: No thanks. (*Lights the cigarette.*)

ERNEST (*as he lights his own*): There's an open window over there . . . In a week everything should be in order out here.

FRANCIS: Well, will the workmen be through then?

ERNEST: Yes, they should be. And then I'll move all the models down below and have an empty studio. And up here the large room will be available so that I can do the honors for you and my other good friends out here. (*Lifts the glass without drinking.*) You don't know how delighted I am to have gotten this cottage out here in Flushing. Just far enough from the city and close enough to you. Thank you, my dear Francis, for helping me get it so well and so quickly. (*They drink.*)

FRANCIS: Are you really planning to keep your job in this firm much longer?

ERNEST: Yes, for the time being. Now that they have doubled my salary, I can really feel secure until I am able to organize my own firm.

FRANCIS: That wasn't the only reason I asked.

ERNEST: Well?

FRANCIS: I was just thinking that your future isn't entirely secure until everything is arranged concerning your divorce. If Norma keeps on being stubborn, it wouldn't hurt if you put a little more distance between you.

ERNEST: Oh, I don't know. I think it's quite the opposite. I have to put it in the hands of a lawyer soon. And then I would need to be available.

FRANCIS: Has she stopped writing to you at the office?

ERNEST: Yes, I returned her last letters unopened.

FRANCIS: At last. That helped—what did I tell you?

ERNEST: I knew very well, Francis, that it was the only way. But I felt it was so brutal, and I still think so. I would gladly have spared her this cruelty, if these daily letters hadn't started an unpleasant suspicion at the office. I *couldn't* spare her.

FRANCIS: Has she never tried to make her way into the laboratory?

ERNEST: Yes, more than once. And given her name, so that everyone knows who she is. She hasn't spared me the public scandal. And she must have thought she knew me well enough to believe that I would avoid a scandal. But painful as it was—I preferred it.

FRANCIS: So she has started to give in?

ERNEST: Give in! (*Shakes his head.*) She waits for me every day when I come from the lab. Sometimes I see her through the window and have time to slip out through the gate to the next street. But many times I have to wait until I am quite certain. Wait until she gets tired of waiting.

FRANCIS: This is an intolerable situation . . . Was she there today?

ERNEST: Yes, yes. Every single day.

FRANCIS: But don't you suspect that she may have found out where you are staying?

ERNEST: No one knows that except the office chief. He will keep it secret from everybody. I can rely on him. But still I have no doubt that I can't live here very long before she does find it out.

FRANCIS: She may have gone to the police.

ERNEST: No, not yet. But I'm sure she has a private detective on my trail.

FRANCIS: I thought she might. Have you noticed one?

ERNEST: Yes, I first noticed the fellow four days ago. I was on my way out here by train and I noticed the man following me to the station. That evening I fooled him. I stayed on to Douglaston and walked quite a distance back here. But then the night before last I saw him poking around the house here when I got home.

FRANCIS (*takes a drink*): I don't know what I would do if I were married to a woman like that.

ERNEST: Tell me, Francis, what would you do?

FRANCIS: It's easier to say it now that we have seen the results. In the first place I would not have moved out of the house as things stood. I would first have used every possible means to force her to divorce me. Not persuasion, I mean. They have no effect on her. No, simply by making her life at home unbearable. Not hesitate to do anything at all within the limits of the law that might drive her away.

ERNEST: I could never do that. To do that I would have to stop distinguishing between right and wrong.

FRANCIS: Exactly—without mercy.

ERNEST: You talk as if you bore illwill to Norma.

FRANCIS: No, I don't bear her any illwill. But I don't like her, and I never have.

ERNEST: Never? Never in the nine years we have been married?

FRANCIS: Never. I have tried to like her, and if I succeeded, it was only on account of you. And it was in spite of the many times I was furious at the way she treated you. If I have managed to conceal this, Ernest, perhaps you will take it as an expression of the consideration I owe you.

ERNEST: And now—now that she is unhappy, why do you say it now?

FRANCIS: I'll tell you why, Ernest. If things should go wrong, I don't want to have to blame myself for not having made my little contribution to save you from a fall, humanly and socially. Now you're smiling. But you won't smile at misfortune when it strikes.

ERNEST: When it strikes, Francis—when doesn't it strike?

FRANCIS: You love this woman. You love her still. If she gets a chance to talk to you, I don't think you will be strong enough to stay out of her clutches. Just think of what it will mean to go back to her again. How can you with your honest, unblemished character resume a marriage which is stained and furrowed by dishonesty and deception? (*Puts his hand on his shoulder.*) Now don't get angry, my dear friend. But you mustn't give in. You must *not* give in.

ERNEST (*gets up*): Do you think I have taken this step without thinking it all the way through? Norma and I have parted, forever. But—well, I don't know. You can't live with a woman for nine years without her having some share in your inmost—

FRANCIS: Habits. Let's just call it habits.

ERNEST: With me it is more than habits. With me it is a longing. Sometimes I wish she were here, and that she could convince me I am doing her an injustice, and that I could kneel down before her and receive her forgiveness. No, Francis, I know it is a weakness, a great weakness—and therefore I stand firm as a rock on my decision.

FRANCIS: It is a weakness I scarcely would have believed you had.

ERNEST: You judge so harshly because you don't know the source of my weakness. It comes from uncertainty. *Am* I doing her an injustice? *Is* my suspicion right? If I had an unshakable certainty that it was right, this weakness would disappear at once.

FRANCIS (*gets up*): Then get that certainty!

ERNEST: How would I go about getting it?

FRANCIS: I don't know . . . But let that be your next, your greatest invention. (*Empties the glass and buttons his jacket.*)

ERNEST (*goes over to the table and empties his glass*): Have a cigar.

FRANCIS (*takes the cigar, makes a hole in the end with a match, and lights it*): You'll be in early tomorrow of course?

ERNEST: Seven-thirty. I'll use the car. I can't resist the pleasure of trying it these first days.

FRANCIS: No, I understand that. But we'll meet at lunch.

55

ERNEST: Yes, and then you'll drive out with me.

FRANCIS: I'll drive out with you. (*They leave through the door left*).

(*The stage is empty a short time. Then a scraping is heard at the bay window on the right, and through the window*)

NORMA (*enters. She steps soundlessly down, walks into the middle of the floor, and sighs*): Thank heavens! (*Looks hastily around the room. Takes off her hat and coat and lays them on the bed. Goes quickly over to the toilet commode and stands a while before the mirror. Strokes her face a couple of times with the tips of her fingers and sighs again. Straightens her hair, lets her powder puff glide over her face, smooths her dress a little, and now has time to look around a little more.*) So this is how he has arranged things for himself. (*Appearing to discover the desk for the first time.*) Doesn't he have more than one room? (*Goes to the door in the rear and opens it carefully. Looks for the switch by the door and turns it on. A glimpse is seen of a room full of all kinds of technical models, machines, conveyor belts, vises, blocks, chemical apparatus, etc.*) Here he works . . . No, I shouldn't. (*Turns off the light and closes the door. Goes over to the bed and caresses the pillow gently with her hand.*) How I love you, Ernest. (*Sits down on the daybed with an expression of weariness and vexation. Sits quite still.*)

(*Ernest opens the door and enters the room, hardly gets time to be surprised at her presence before*)

NORMA (*runs towards him with her arms outstretched*): At last, at last—

ERNEST (*grips both her wrists and pushes her away*): How did you get in here?

NORMA (*again trying to approach him*): Ernest, my beloved— my darling—you mustn't push me away. (*Complaining.*) You don't know how I have suffered.

ERNEST: Have I suffered less? I tell you immediately that if you wish to start a conversation between us, you will succeed only if you don't make any attempt to touch me. Why do you have to use such miserable weapons? Sit down on the daybed, and I will listen calmly to what you have to say.

NORMA: Take me in your arms, Ernest dear. Then I can speak confidently with you. Otherwise I know you are angry at me.

ERNEST: And if I am angry at you, by what law of the human soul can you expect that I will take you in my arms before that anger is extinguished? Sit down on the daybed—or get out of here!

(*Norma sits on the daybed. Ernest takes a chair nearby and sits down.*)

NORMA: Oh, if you only knew how I have suffered! Every single night I have strayed around in the rooms at home like a mad person, back and forth, back and forth. Thirteen endless nights. And every single day I have waited for you by the door of the laboratory after working hours, and twice I had to suffer the outrage that you denied your wife admission. Oh God in heaven, there isn't a torture I haven't suffered.

ERNEST: Yes, you didn't spare me the scandal.

NORMA: Thirteen endless days! Thirteen endless days!

ERNEST: I bore my sorrow in silence for nineteen nights. And after that came thirteen more. Nineteen and thirteen are thirty-two.

NORMA: Believe me, Ernest, I have learned to understand now what you have had to suffer. And it is to tell you this that I made all these efforts to speak with you. (*Gets up and starts for him.*)

ERNEST (*with decisive emotion*): Sit down!

NORMA (*sits down again*): I have been vile toward you, Ernest. But not on purpose. Only in thoughtlessness. Now, afterwards, I have seen it all. It wasn't right of me—it was unforgivably thoughtless of me to give you reason to think I had violated your trust. But I also know in my heart of hearts that I have not done so.

ERNEST: What is it you call "giving me reason to think you had violated my trust"?

NORMA: When I noticed that my association with Mr. Rattigan displeased you, I came with a long and zealous defense of my need for luxuries. Instead of trying to understand what you would think, how you would feel, and taking that into consideration. Instead of thanking you doubly for your efforts to give me the pleasure I had had so recently. That is the thoughtlessness I can't forgive myself.

ERNEST: I can forgive you for that—if that was all.

NORMA: Thanks, Ernest, thanks. You are so good.

ERNEST: If that was all—I said.

NORMA: Has it never occurred to you that you might be wronging me? When you sit there alone with your thoughts, have you never seen me as a poor abandoned woman, lashed by your suspicions as by a storm? Has it never occurred to you that you could be mistaken?

ERNEST: Now you are speaking calmly, Norma. There you see. We can talk better as soon as you just take things a little more calmly.

NORMA (*with a sigh of relief*): How lovely it is to hear you speak this way. It is like a warm breath of air caressing my cheeks. I'll be calm. Then we can talk much better, can't we?

ERNEST: I just said so.

NORMA: Yes, that's right. And now I ask you once more: has uncertainty never visited you? Have you never doubted whether your accusation was supported by facts? Do you remember what you said once last year when we read in the paper that all twelve jurors condemned a man for murder, and Mr. Robert Belford refused to pronounce judgment immediately because he doubted that he was guilty? Then you said something I can never forget. You said that doubt was the conscience of justice.

ERNEST: Norma, of all the things you have said about this affair, there is only one that has stuck in my mind. On the day I left home, you said to me "You think everything is much worse than it is." If I do this, Norma, it is your fault.

NORMA: How is it my fault, Ernest? Tell me that. For heaven's sake tell me.

ERNEST: From the start you have acted very unwisely. You stubbornly denied the trifles that I immediately saw must have taken place between you and Mr. Rattigan. In this way you strengthened my suspicion that more serious things had happened. If you had openly admitted, as soon as it came up, that you had flirted a little with Mr. Rattigan, then your open admission would have corresponded exactly to what I myself had discovered. Then my suspicions would have vanished like dew in the sun. She's not trying to fool me, I would have thought; it's all relatively harmless. Don't you see that yourself?

NORMA: Yes—well—what do you call "flirting"?

ERNEST: Whatever happened between you in Florida. An innocent mutual attraction between a man and a woman who find that they have common interests, feelings, maybe even a common outlook. Such an attraction quite naturally finds its expression in intimate glances, in long handclasps as between good friends, in stolen kisses on the cheek or the hair now and then—things that are forgotten as soon as they happen. It is all so harmless and natural that "I could have seen it all," as you yourself said. And one more thing: words, warm, beautiful, admiring words that all women need to hear. What would it all have been but mere trifles, if you had not done everything to conceal it from me? This was what aroused my suspicions.

NORMA: But I have not tried to conceal anything from you,

ERNEST. You have found the explanation yourself. All that took place between Mr. Rattigan and me was just that kind of mere trifles, which I would have found it ridiculous to confess.

ERNEST: Quite ridiculous—if only you had not by your silence lost the chance to regain my complete confidence. But I can see that this makes no difference to you.

NORMA: You are wrong, Ernest. There is nothing I would have preferred more than regaining your confidence. It is true that I may have flirted quite superficially with Mr. Rattigan—but you won't believe that this has nothing to do with my feelings.

ERNEST: Yes, I am anxious to believe you, and if you had told me right away—

NORMA (*eagerly*): Heavens, a person can flirt with a man for an evening without—

ERNEST: A thousand evenings, Norma, a thousand evenings. Were you really afraid that I would have been angry if you had told me you had kissed Mr. Rattigan once? You would have eased my mind by telling me.

NORMA: You can call it kissing, if you wish. I can tell you exactly what happened. I don't *wish* to conceal anything from you. One evening he came into my room at the hotel, and I saw that he was struggling with something. I knew that he was in love with me—he had told me that. Then suddenly he fell on his knees before me, weeping. I felt so sorry for him, seeing him cry like a baby, and—

ERNEST: And what?

NORMA: And—I bent down over him.

ERNEST: And then?

NORMA: And then I straightened up, walked away from him, and asked him to leave the room.

ERNEST: Without kissing him?

NORMA: Kissing him—I didn't kiss him at all. Oh, I gave him

60

a kiss on the cheek when I said goodbye. I told him that he would never see me again if he kept troubling me with his stupid declarations of love. I must grant him that his behavior toward me since that evening has always been polite and correct. Always . . . Now I have confessed the whole thing to you exactly as it was—and now you sit there condemning me in your thoughts. I can see it on you. I knew it, I knew it.

ERNEST: No, no, not for a moment. (*While he is struggling with a new idea.*) Now, Norma, that confession wasn't so terribly difficult.

NORMA: No, not now. But you have never spoken to me with such understanding as you have this evening. If you had always been like this toward me, I would never have concealed anything from you. But I was so afraid that you would look severely on this thing. And it was probably not quite right of me to continue associating with him when I knew he loved me.

ERNEST: Well—how could you help that?

NORMA: No, but anyway. Now it doesn't matter. For now he's over it long ago.

(*Ernest goes over to the daybed and sits down beside her.*)

NORMA (*throws her arms around him and lays her head against his chest with a long, happy sigh*): Oh-h—thank you, darling. Thank you for sitting down beside me. I am so happy, so happy.

ERNEST: Will you tell me one thing, Norma, which I want to ask you about?

NORMA: Anything, anything, beloved, I'll tell you anything. Just so you will keep me in your arms. That is the only place I feel calm and secure. Yes, like that. Now I live again. Now I'll close my eyes and listen to you speak.

ERNEST: Here we sit, the two of us. There is nothing that separates our hearts. Everything we think and say to each other at this moment will build our lives out of their ruins. Therefore we will both remember to let every one of our words pass through the forge of truth. As we are sitting here, it is easy for us to show each other full confidence.

NORMA: Keep talking—it is so lovely to listen to your words.

ERNEST (*draws her closer to him*): In this way we can be secure. No truth, however bitter, can do us any harm. It is all the other things, the compromises, the lack of trust in each other, that seek to part us and destroy our happiness.

NORMA: But after this not even that shall part us. I promise you that. No compromises. No lack of trust, nothing on earth.

ERNEST: Norma—have you belonged to Mr. Rattigan with all your soul and all your body?

NORMA (*starts out of his arms, as before a death-dealing blow, looks him in the eye, but gets no explanation from his expression, which is full of sincerity and gentleness*): I knew it, I knew it. As soon as I told you the truth, you only suspected me of something else and worse. I knew it would only feed your suspiciousness if I told you. And then you reproached me for preferring to be silent. It makes no difference what I do, it is always wrong. I knew it, I knew it.

ERNEST: Norma—think of your and my future. I just beg you to tell me the truth, quietly and without mincing words. Did you give yourself to him? Yes or no!

NORMA: Are you out of your mind?

ERNEST: Yes—or no!

NORMA: No, no, no! A thousand times no!

ERNEST: Then my last hope is gone.

NORMA: What do you mean?

ERNEST (*goes over to the desk and leans against the edge of it*): My hope of ever again being happy in our marriage—this answer has extinguished it. I see life ahead as a wasteland, where nothing can grow. I am alone, quite alone—as

I have been these days. You are alone, quite alone—as you have been these days. Every bond that held us together is burnt—and the ashes are in my hand.

NORMA (*getting up*): What in the world is wrong with you, Ernest? You frighten me. You are making me think that I am alone with a madman.

ERNEST (*with a faint smile*): You needn't worry, Norma.

NORMA: I needn't worry! When I hear you saying that all your hope is gone because I have not belonged to any man but you, because I have *not* been unfaithful to you!

ERNEST: How differently we two love!

NORMA: I don't understand you—won't you please explain what you mean?

ERNEST (*returns to the daybed and sits down*): No explanation can help us now. It is all over.

NORMA (*sits down beside him*): No, you mustn't say that. I would like to understand you—I have no higher wish. And I'll succeed, you just see.

ERNEST: I don't believe it. But I won't leave you until I've given you a full explanation of my actions. You have a right to that—whether you understand them or not. (*Puts his arm around her shoulder.*) I have loved you, Norma . . . (*Norma leans her head against his chest.*)

ERNEST: I have loved you—very differently and far more deeply than you have seen or tried to see. And I have always considered your love for me as the only precious treasure I had. You did not always notice it, I'll grant—and now I can tell you why. I was careless with my treasure, because I was proud of it. It was like a priceless jewel that one is pleased to treat lightly in order to make others think that one is richer than one is. I was careless with it—until you returned from Florida, and I was afraid I had lost it. Since that time I have been thinking and thinking. I thought about the coldness you showed me, a thoughtlessness that sometimes took the form of out-and-out enmity. What was its source? Yes, you were right: I did suffer from jealousy. All the time, while I was at home. But when I was alone, when I had moved away from you—when everything that was delightful in your being had turned to memories of something I could neither see nor hear nor touch, memories without flesh and blood—then the jealousy vanished, and was forgotten, just as a small accident is forgotten for a horrible tragedy. It was more than forgotten. It came back to me in a new shape, as the last hope for my happiness. Do you understand me, Norma?

NORMA: I have understood everything you said, every single point—except this about your jealousy. I don't understand that.

ERNEST: Thanks for your frankness, Norma. The explanation is coming. The tragedy I spoke of was the only explanation there could be of your behavior. Then began for the first time a struggle of a thousand forces in my brain. The struggle over how I could win back your love. If you had come back from Florida *without* any other man's having captured your emotions, if you showed such thoughtless lack of consideration *without* your heart's being full of love for another—then it had to be because your heart was empty, because your love was dead. Then the struggle was hopeless . . . But if you had fallen in love— (*Interrupts himself.*)

NORMA: What then, Ernest, what then?

ERNEST: Do you still understand me?

NORMA: Yes, I do. What were you going to say?

ERNEST: If you had fallen in love with another man for a time, not just in a kind of superficial and silly way, and your love had been sincere and deep and pure, full of a passion that justified it, then I could not only have understood the reason for the change in you, I could have taken up the battle in the hope of winning you back, winning you forever.

64

What happens to jealousy when our whole life's happiness is at stake? I believed in this possibility until you came here this evening, but I was wrong. Nobody else has supplanted your love for me in your heart. It died a natural death inside you.

NORMA: No, no, Ernest, you mustn't say these frightful words.

ERNEST: Why don't you say anything?

NORMA: I? . . . What can I say?

ERNEST: No, what *can* you say? Not a word. Not a word can you say. You know the whole thing is true.

NORMA: No, you mustn't get up! Do you hear! I am so frightened.

ERNEST: Why are you frightened?

NORMA: I don't know . . . Ernest, I love you.

ERNEST: Norma, do you remember our nights after you returned from Florida? Do you remember how you avoided me, how you hurt me by thinking it was necessary to avoid me, and could find no other excuse except that you were tired? Tired after two months' separation from me! That was because your love was dead.

(*Norma puts her hands before her face.*)

ERNEST: How I have loved you, cold woman! With a reverence that was too sacred to have a name. When I kissed your lips, I did not kiss your mouth. I was bending my knee to you, and bringing my adoration to that threshold which your and my soul would some day cross in the shape of a little child.

(*Norma is overwhelmed by his words, throws herself on the edge of the daybed as she sobs loudly.*)

ERNEST: Yes, go ahead and cry, Norma. Bear your and my grief to the grave at which you are sorrowing. You were faithful to me. But when did unfaithfulness ever treat anyone more harshly than your faithfulness has treated me?

Before I plumbed the depths of my passion, I cried in a loud voice: let not unfaithfulness enter my temple! Now I whisper in a child's voice: a thousand times rather unfaithfulness than to find the temple closed, and then when one opens it, to find it empty. He who is faithful, but without love—*his* treason is the greatest.

NORMA (*rises, but immediately sinks weakly down to him*): Can you forgive me—I can no longer conceal it from you. Cannot and will not.

ERNEST: You—you are concealing nothing from me.

NORMA: I have loved Edward Rattigan.

ERNEST: You—you cannot love anyone.

NORMA: I have loved him—until the day you left home. *He* can speak of my love being dead. Not you. I don't know if I have understood you, Ernest; I have tried. Now I beg you try to understand *me*. You said earlier that I had not always noticed how rich your love was. No, I haven't. You were stingy with your words of love, like a miser brooding on his gold. You also called my love a treasure and said you had been careless with it. I felt it all too often. If it *is* an excuse that this man thawed out those springs of passion which had frozen up in marital habits, then I'll mention this excuse. But not really for *my* sake. If you forgive me, I have nothing to regret. Some wise man has said that it is only through sin we attain perfection. It is through my misstep that I now love you as purely and deeply as any woman can love.

ERNEST: Are you sure that you know yourself, Norma? What was your misstep? When you gave yourself to him, didn't you hold back some of your passion, so that you were neither wholly his nor wholly mine?

NORMA: No, I can't divide myself between two. That is why I avoided all your tenderness. It was not in order to hurt you needlessly. It was because I had to be honest with myself. It was no superficial flirt, Ernest. It was a passion, which consumed my feelings. I gave him just as few days of my life as I have given you many years. Now you know everything.

ERNEST (*rising*): Yes, now I know everything. As far as that goes, everything I knew before. No more. No less.

NORMA: I thought you would hold me tight and be good to me?

ERNEST: This is the only time in my life I have not been honest with you, Norma.

(*Norma's features stiffen.*)

ERNEST: All this time since I left home, I have been determined that if we met again, I would force this confession from your lips. It was the only way I could save myself.

NORMA: Save yourself—from what?

ERNEST: From you. From your deception.

NORMA (*gets up*): Have you been sitting here, holding me close, luring me to your heart, fooling me into believing you, under the guise of love and nobility—all with the sole purpose of performing a highly refined deception? I would never have suspected you of such an ignoble betrayal.

ERNEST: If I may grant myself a bit of justification, it would be that the betrayal you have committed is a good deal more ignoble. You concealed the truth with the sole purpose of deceiving me. I concealed the truth with the sole purpose of revealing the truth.

NORMA: Never, never as long as I live will I forgive you for this—this calculated meanness. Yes, now I see the whole thing. You did not use honorable weapons. First you made me weak, set me to crying, and then you let loving words fall like a whiplash on my soul. That is how you did it. First you paralyzed my arm, and then you stole the weapon from my hand. Lies, lies the whole thing.

ERNEST: I happen to have a different conception of the relation between truth and lies, between love and trifling. You were to be allowed to deceive me, and then to wash away my suspicions by tears and embraces. But I was not to be allowed to use my intelligence to see through those tears and those embraces and look right into the heart of your lie. This is what you cannot forget as long as you live. I swear to you that this evening is the last time we will speak together in our lives.

NORMA: What are you planning to do?

ERNEST: I plan to make you understand that from this moment all association between us is definitely at an end. And now—now I beg you to leave me alone.

NORMA: I shall not burden you again with my tears or my embraces—but I *am* your wife, and I will not allow myself to be chased away.

ERNEST: What are you saying? A woman who deceives her husband? Fine, then I'll bring the matter to court.

NORMA: Do you think any court can force me to divorce my husband if I don't want to? You have no proofs.

ERNEST: But you yourself have confessed.

NORMA: Where are the witnesses to this confession? I'll say you're lying. You lied to me before. Or I'll say something else that is more effective.

ERNEST: What is that?

NORMA: That will come up when the time is ripe.

ERNEST: What are *you* planning to do, Norma? Do you intend to spend the night here?

NORMA: Yes—if you won't come home with me.

(*Ernest opens the clothes closet and takes out a suitcase. Walks over to the desk, opens the drawers, and puts various letters and the like into the suitcase, plus some of the things on the table.*)

NORMA: I won't let you go, Ernest. If you plan to leave me

now, I'll go with you. You can't prevent it. I won't let you go, do you hear, I won't let you go.

(*Ernest picks up the suitcase without closing it, so that the long straps drag on the floor, and walks toward the door in the rear.*)

NORMA (*runs to the door*): If you are leaving, you'll take me with you.

ERNEST (*with perfect restraint*): Will you please step aside from the door, so I can get out?

NORMA: No, not without me.

(*Ernest puts down the suitcase, pulls out the straps, takes Norma and leads her over to the chair before the toilet commode.*)

NORMA: What are you doing?

ERNEST: Don't worry. I won't hurt you. (*Places her in the chair and ties her by the straps. Tightens one strap around her arms and through the spokes of the chair, the other over her knees. While he is doing this, they exchange the following two speeches.*)

NORMA: Are you laying hands on a woman?

ERNEST: You have your tears—I have my strength. These are a man's and a woman's most basic weapons. But I won't let you wait long in this position. Twenty minutes at the most. I'll drive over to McLean's, and as soon as I get there, he will come here and release you. Then you are free, and I will be, too. I will then have disappeared from your life. I'll go away—far, far into the world.

(*Norma weeps quietly.*)

ERNEST (*takes a couple of steps away*): You have your one hundred and fifty thousand dollars in the bank. For the time being that should suffice. When you want to make further arrangements about the divorce, you can turn to Mr. Posner. Everything else I'll arrange later. If you feel that my forgiveness means anything to you, you may expect to hear from me one single time. Perhaps, I say. For it can't come before I have stopped loving you. (*Takes the suitcase.*) Goodbye, Norma. (*Leaves by the door rear.*)

(*Norma struggles with the chair, but soon discovers how heavy it is. Then she appears to fall into a state of coma. The rustling heard from the neighboring room does not disturb her. But suddenly her eyes light up at a thought that occurs to her. As Ernest is heard closing the door out to the hallway behind him, she laughs. She sends crystal clear waves of laughter out into the room, louder and clearer as his steps grow fainter. She listens between each laugh. She laughs more and more weakly, until the door on the left opens. Her laughter has called him back. Ernest enters and remains standing on the threshold. Norma pays no attention to him, but goes on laughing.*)

ERNEST (*puts down his suitcase and walks over to the chair*): What's the matter with you, Norma?

NORMA: Why don't you leave?

ERNEST: I had left, I was on my way down the stairs. But then I heard you laughing. What's the matter with you?

NORMA: And then you came back—then you didn't dare but come back.

ERNEST: I thought maybe something was wrong with you. I don't know, but I felt it was uncanny to hear you and then leave you this way.

NORMA: Tied up?

ERNEST: No, laughing.

NORMA: There is something I would like to say to you before you leave, since you have come back. Something that will overthrow all your plans. Something that will please you. Something I have the right to let you know.

ERNEST: What is that?

NORMA: For you *have* decided to leave, haven't you?

ERNEST: Decided . . . I am just waiting to hear what you want to say—if you think it is necessary.

NORMA: Good . . . I promise you that what I tell you now will not be accompanied either by tears or any personal reproaches on my part. I shall tell you the naked facts and nothing else. In return I demand that you release me from the bondage you have subjected me to. I want to speak to you as a free woman, as your wife, and not as a slave in chains.

ERNEST: I'll release you, Norma. But if you fail me this time, you'll suffer the consequences.

NORMA: If you still want to leave after I have told you, you won't need to do so. I'll leave myself, and you won't see me again.

(*Ernest unties the straps.*)

NORMA (*gets up, walks over to the daybed, and sits down*): In the meantime, please sit down.

(*Ernest takes out a chair and is seated.*)

NORMA (*with a bright smile*): Do you know why I laughed? I was sure you would come back when you heard me laugh. If not, I wouldn't have let you go. For the last twenty minutes I have been waiting for this moment with a wild yearning. Have you never looked forward so much to doing something that you postponed it to the last moment, to the very brink of possibility, so to speak, just to be able to enjoy your anticipation to the utmost?

ERNEST: What do you want to tell me?

NORMA: Now listen carefully—You think you have been very clever this evening. You constructed a trap for me in an unusually subtle way. You set it for me, and now you think you have caught me in it. It has not occurred to you that I might have been even more clever than you. Do you think I have been married to you for nine years without

71

knowing that you never would forgive me if I had really done what I confessed this evening? But it is true: For a moment I did believe that your love was deep enough so that you had the will to forgive all. Therefore I listened to you, let you think you had caught me, drew the bow as high as possible. I told you more and more. I wanted to know how much you loved me—and then, then when I had your forgiveness, I looked forward so joyfully to telling you the truth. To telling you that the whole thing was a lie, that it was all done to test your love. I looked forward to being able to sweep away your baseless suspicion in this way once and for all. But—your forgiveness did not come. That was a disappointment. It angered me. And so I continued the game. If you had the right to use any means in order to discover whether your wife was unfaithful to you, then I had the right to use any means to discover how much my husband loved me. Which of us was the cleverest? I have never loved Mr. Rattigan, never kissed him, never been his. That man means nothing to me now and never has, not more than the table over there.

ERNEST (*leaps to his feet and rushes frenziedly back and forth on the floor*): God in heaven, what a conscience! Is no falsehood so mean, no lie so barefaced, that you are not ashamed to adopt it? So this is how you deceived me? Not a jot more hesitantly than this. With precisely the same coldbloodedness as the one with which you are now telling me this lie as you sit there. Go away and never let me see you again!

(*Norma goes over to him and puts her hand on his arm.*)

ERNEST: Don't touch me—you whore!

NORMA: You have no right to fling that word in my face.

ERNEST: Where can I go to be reconciled to my fate? Where on earth can I get forgiveness for having given you my sincere love? You are worse than the whore in the street, a thousand, thousand times worse. In her sincerity she is faithful, in her faithlessness she is sincere. No one mistakes her. But you—I have taken you into the sacredness of my heart, and you have soiled it for ever. (*His voice trembles in fury as he leans against the table and grips the edge with his hands, while he tries to restrain the burning emotions of his heart.*) And now go—get out of my life!

NORMA (*goes over to him, throws her arms around his neck*): I won't leave you, Ernest. You know you are doing me a wrong . . . You do love me.

ERNEST: I love you! . . . How do I love you . . . This is how I love you. (*Fumbles across the table, in his confusion seizes an iron paperweight, and hits her on the head with it.*) (*Norma falls, unconscious from the blow and without making a sound, before his feet.*)

ERNEST (*rushing back and forth in unbridled emotion—with short, jerky breathing*): That's how I love you, yes. That's how I love you. (*Stops some distance away.*) Why did you tease me like that? (*Pacing some more.*) Why did you throw your arms around me at the same moment you had maddened me with grief and anger? . . . Otherwise I wouldn't have done it . . . (*Goes closer to her and stops.*) Does it hurt very much? . . . (*Goes over to her.*) Norma, does it hurt very much? . . . Norma! . . . Norma! . . . (*Falls on one knee and bends over her. Takes her hand in alarm and feels her pulse. Calls with a loud voice.*) Norma, Norma, Norma, Norma! (*Puts his ear to her heart. Slowly gets to his feet, pale as a corpse, with every feature of his face frozen. Tries to take a step, then sinks down, overwhelmed, on the floor beside her.*) Why did you torture me so long, oh my beloved? . . . Of all the things that could happen, this is what I wanted the least. (*Looks up with imploring eyes.*) Did I really do it? . . . Who was so ill-disposed to our love? My little girl, my little girl . . . (*His tears fall on her face, his head sinks down on her bosom. His whole body is shaken by sobs. Then he lifts her head up from the floor and presses a kiss on her forehead. Gets to his feet, takes her in his arms, and carries her over to the bed. He crosses her hands on her breast, kisses them, and spreads her coat over her. Staggers to the table, stares at the paperweight, touches it, but immediately pulls back his hand. Stares into space.*) How lucky you are . . . How lucky *you* are! . . .

CURTAIN

PUBLISHED IN THE NORDIC TRANSLATION SERIES

FROM DENMARK

H. C. Branner, *Two Minutes of Silence*. Selected short stories, translated by Vera Lindholm Vance, with an introduction by Richard B. Vowles. 1966.

Tom Kristensen, *Havoc*. *Hærværk*, translated by Carl Malmberg, with an introduction by Børge Gedsø Madsen. 1968.

Jacob Paludan, *Jørgen Stein*. Translated by Carl Malmberg, with an introduction by P. M. Mitchell. 1966.

FROM FINLAND

Hagar Olsson, *The Woodcarver and Death*. *Träsnidaren och döden*, translated from the Swedish by George C. Schoolfield. 1965.

Toivo Pekkanen, *My Childhood*. *Lapsuuteni*, translated by

Alan Blair, with an introduction by Thomas Warburton. 1966.

F. E. Sillanpää, *People in the Summer Night. Ihmiset suviyössä,* translated by Alan Blair, with an introduction by Thomas Warburton. 1966.

FROM ICELAND

Fire and Ice: Three Icelandic Plays, with introductions by Einar Haugen. Jóhan Sigurjónsson, *The Wish (Galdra-Loftur),* translated by Einar Haugen. Davið Stefánsson, *The Golden Gate (Gullna hliðið),* translated by G. M. Gathorne-Hardy. Agnar Thórðarson, *Atoms and Madams (Kjarnorka og kvenhylli),* translated by Einar Haugen. 1967.

Gunnar Gunnarsson, *The Black Cliffs. Svartfugl,* translated from the Danish by Cecil Wood, with an introduction by Richard N. Ringler. 1967.

Guðmundur Kamban, *We Murderers. Vi Mordere,* translated from the Danish by Einar Haugen, with an introduction by D. E. Askey. 1970.

Halldor Laxness, *World Light. Heimsljós,* translated by Magnus Magnusson. 1969.

FROM NORWAY

Johan Falkberget, *The Fourth Night Watch. Den fjerde nattevakt,* translated by Ronald G. Popperwell. 1968.

Aksel Sandemose, *The Werewolf. Varulven,* translated by Gustaf Lannestock, with an introduction by Harald S. Næss. 1966.

Tarjei Vesaas, *The Great Cycle. Det store spelet,* translated by Elizabeth Rokkan, with an introduction by Harald S. Næss. 1967.

Tage Aurell, *Rose of Jericho and Other Stories. Berättelser,* translated by Martin Allwood, with an introduction by Eric O. Johannesson. 1968.

Karin Boye, *Kallocain.* Translated by Gustaf Lannestock, with an introduction by Richard B. Vowles. 1966.

Peder Sjögren, *Bread of Love. Kärlekens bröd,* translated by Richard B. Vowles. 1965.